Blue Dream

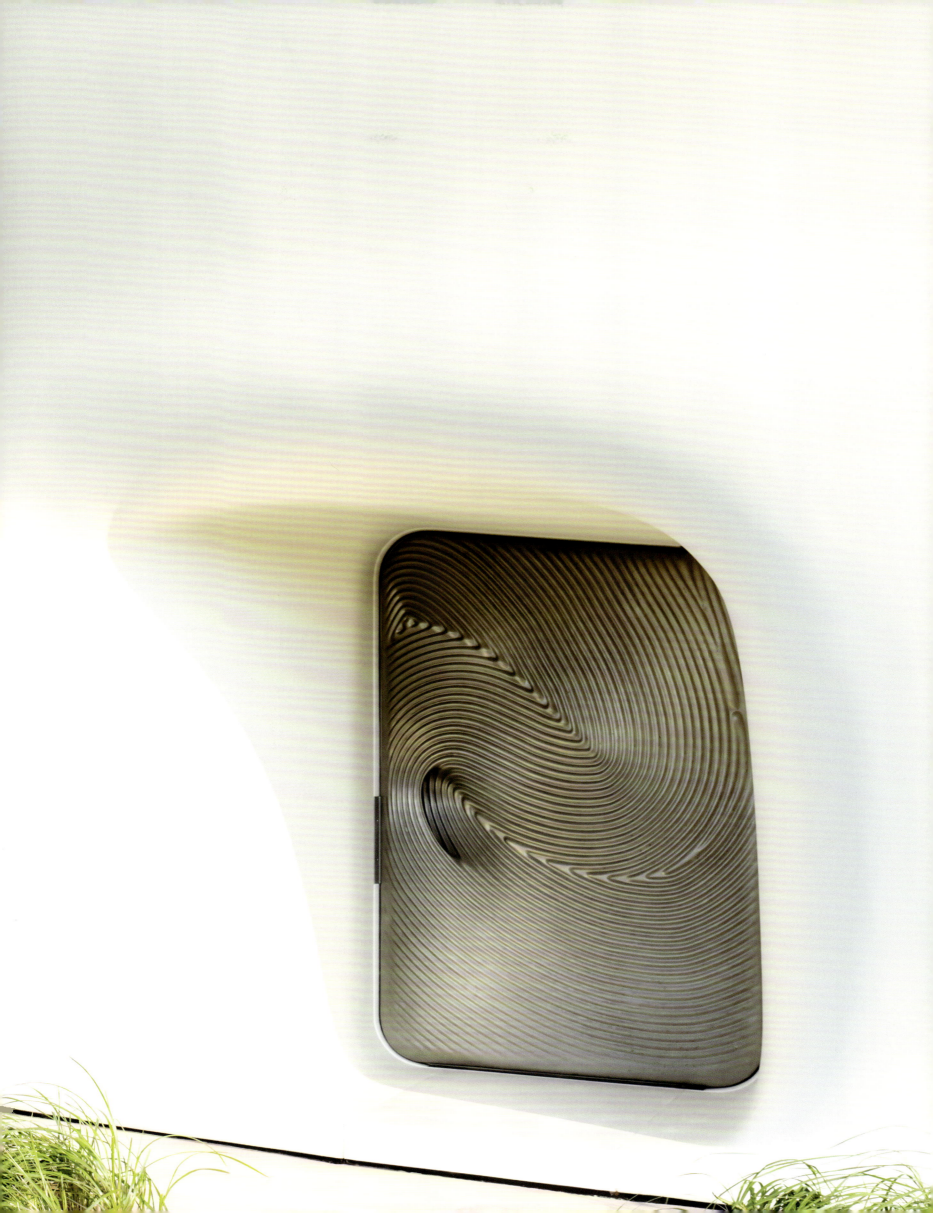

Paul Goldberger

BLUE DREAM AND THE LEGACY OF MODERNISM IN THE HAMPTONS

a house by Diller Scofidio + Renfro
with a photographic portfolio by Iwan Baan

DelMonico Books • D.A.P. New York

CONTENTS

- 17 To build a house like no other...
- 33 For a love of design
- 57 Where modernism flourished
- 71 The question of an architect
- 93 Starting over
- 105 Designing a structural experiment
- 129 A material breakthrough
- 177 *Gesamtkunstwerk* on the Atlantic Double Dunes
- 233 Moving toward completion
- 261 Making modernism new again

- 273 A note from the author
- 277 Diller Scofidio + Renfro studio and Blue Dream consultants
- 278 Contributors
- 279 Image credits

OPPOSITE
Katherine Bernhardt, Blue Dream,
black India ink on paper, 2017

for Julie Reyes Taubman

TO BUILD
A HOUSE LIKE
NO OTHER...

The complex relationship of architects, clients, and builders in the creation of houses has been explored for almost as long as people have been writing about buildings, from the treatises of Palladio in the 16th century to novels (and films) like *Mr. Blandings Builds His Dream House* in the 20th. But it too rarely makes its way into standard architectural history, where it is the finished object, not the process by which it takes form, that gets the attention. Not least of the reasons for writing this book is to open the door to a greater sense of the process by which a design and then a finished structure come into being, to show that no design, whatever its origins, ever emerges fully developed like Diana from the head of Zeus. It comes gradually, in fits and starts, sometimes with setbacks and convoluted twists and turns, and both client and builder invariably play critical roles, along with the architect, in making any house what it is.

Blue Dream is not a typical house in any way. Even if some of the ups and downs of its saga—delays, cost overruns, changes during construction—are common to many houses, the particulars here are not common at all. Blue Dream was designed for clients with an exceptional passion for art and architecture, an unusual degree of connoisseurship, the means to collect extraordinary examples of modern design, and the determination to create a house like no other, a house they hoped might take its place among the notable private houses of its time. Such ambitious goals require an unusual architect, and clients Julia Reyes Taubman and Robert Taubman—known to their friends as Julie and Bobby—embarked on a long and complicated search process with multiple false starts. Ultimately, they selected a firm whose founding partners were the first architects ever to have won a MacArthur 'genius grant', and who were recognized internationally for their avant-garde museums, civic and institutional buildings, and projects like the High Line in New York, though they had never completed a private residence. The stage was set for an unusual collaboration in which both client and architect were exceptionally motivated and determined to create something extraordinary, even unique, but they began with little sense of precisely what that would be. The builder was far more experienced, but just as unusual: he was the rare contractor who takes pride in marrying his own practical instincts to the creative imagination of architects and sees his mission as enabling innovative structures to be built.

The location of Blue Dream—East Hampton—is in every way another character in this story. It is an oceanfront community at the east end of Long Island which has long combined elements of a manicured resort town for well-to-do urbanites with a tradition of welcoming avant-garde artists and architects. In recent years, as the town has become more and more expensive, it has lost some of the edge that led painters like Jackson Pollock and Willem de Kooning to settle there, Robert Motherwell to commission the French architect Pierre Chareau to build him a house and studio there, and forward-looking clients to commission architects like Charles Gwathmey and Richard Meier to build some of their most important early houses there. Part of the story of Blue Dream is the story of the place itself and how this house reinvigorates the avant-garde history of the community, making East Hampton—a town in which modern architecture thrived a generation or more ago—once again a place in which new and inventive forms of design might flourish.

But most of all, Blue Dream is a story of architectural ambition. Julie and Robert Taubman wanted to build a house that would express both their love for a specific place and their more general, wide-ranging passion and excitement about the whole notion of architectural experience. They entrusted the architects Diller Scofidio + Renfro to realize their dream, and in time, they did, producing a house that pushed their own widely admired oeuvre in new directions, recalling a time when modernism in the Hamptons was more a quest for structural and spatial innovation than an expression of luxurious elegance. In the end, the house the Taubmans built is important in three distinct ways: as a significant event in the architectural history of East Hampton, as a notable chapter in the development of Diller Scofidio + Renfro's work, and as a major statement in the long history of distinguished and architecturally ambitious modern houses.

Why would someone choose to build a house like nothing else that had been built before? Some of it is the exhilaration of pushing design in a new direction. As with scientific research or financial investing, the greater the risk, the higher the potential reward. The more ambitious the design, the greater the challenge, but also the greater the opportunity. There are relatively few books devoted to the architecture of a single house, but what is clear if you read any of them is that they are stories about clients as much as about architects. Fallingwater, Frank Lloyd Wright's masterpiece of 1937, has been the subject of several books; so has Mies van der Rohe's Edith Farnsworth House of 1951, Frank Lloyd Wright's Robie House of 1909, Le Corbusier's Villa Savoye of 1929, Philip Johnson's Glass House of 1949—all of which can be truly said to have shaped the architecture of the 20th century. Extraordinary private houses are not unique to modern times. There are also books about Thomas Jefferson's Monticello, George Washington's Mount Vernon, Andrea Palladio's Villa Rotunda, and the London townhouse of John Soane which became Sir John Soane's Museum. Each of these houses is a work of architecture that affected the culture of its time and still holds sway over the architectural imagination. They are great works of art, and once they have been made, it is hard to envision a world in which they do not exist.

It is far too soon to know whether Blue Dream will have a similar impact. We know, however, that without Edgar Kaufmann's determination and belief in Frank Lloyd Wright, there would have been no Fallingwater; without Edith Farnsworth, there would have been no Edith Farnsworth House (though she came at times to wish that had been the case, given her troubled relationship with the architect whose masterwork bears her name, but that is another story). Thomas Jefferson, John Soane, and Philip Johnson were their own clients, of course, but Frederick C. Robie was a young businessman who wanted Frank Lloyd Wright to build him a light-filled modern house whose interior would feel more open than the conventional houses of the era, and Pierre and Eugénie Savoye were a sophisticated Parisian couple who came to Le Corbusier and gave him relatively free rein in designing a country house for them. What all of these people had in common was a certainty that they would not be comfortable in a house like other houses. They wanted something made for them that would be different from anything that had been made before.

So, too, with the Taubmans. Julie Taubman had a relationship to design and architecture that made her want to play a role in the creation of a house that would not only shelter her family, but also make a contribution to the history of design, which had long been her passion. The house the Taubmans built would be in every way a collaboration between them, the architects Diller Scofidio + Renfro, the builder Ed Bulgin, landscape architect Michael Boucher, designer Michael Lewis, who assisted Julie in completing the interiors, and other artists, designers, and craftspeople whose work was commissioned specifically for it.

Many years ago, an interviewer asked the architect Louis Kahn if he preferred clients who told him exactly what they wanted, or clients who left the design process entirely up to him. Kahn thought for a moment and said that he did not like either type, since the clients who specified everything seemed to want to design the house themselves, and the ones who said little gave him no ideas to work with, no starting point for collaboration. What he wanted, Kahn said, was the client "who knows what he aspires to."

The Taubmans knew what they aspired to. They wanted to create a work of architecture that would be like nothing else that had been built, a house that would exhilarate them and comfort them at the same time, and that would feel as if it were made only for the dunes beside the Atlantic Ocean. They wanted a house that would enhance the experience of living. This is the story of how that house came to be.

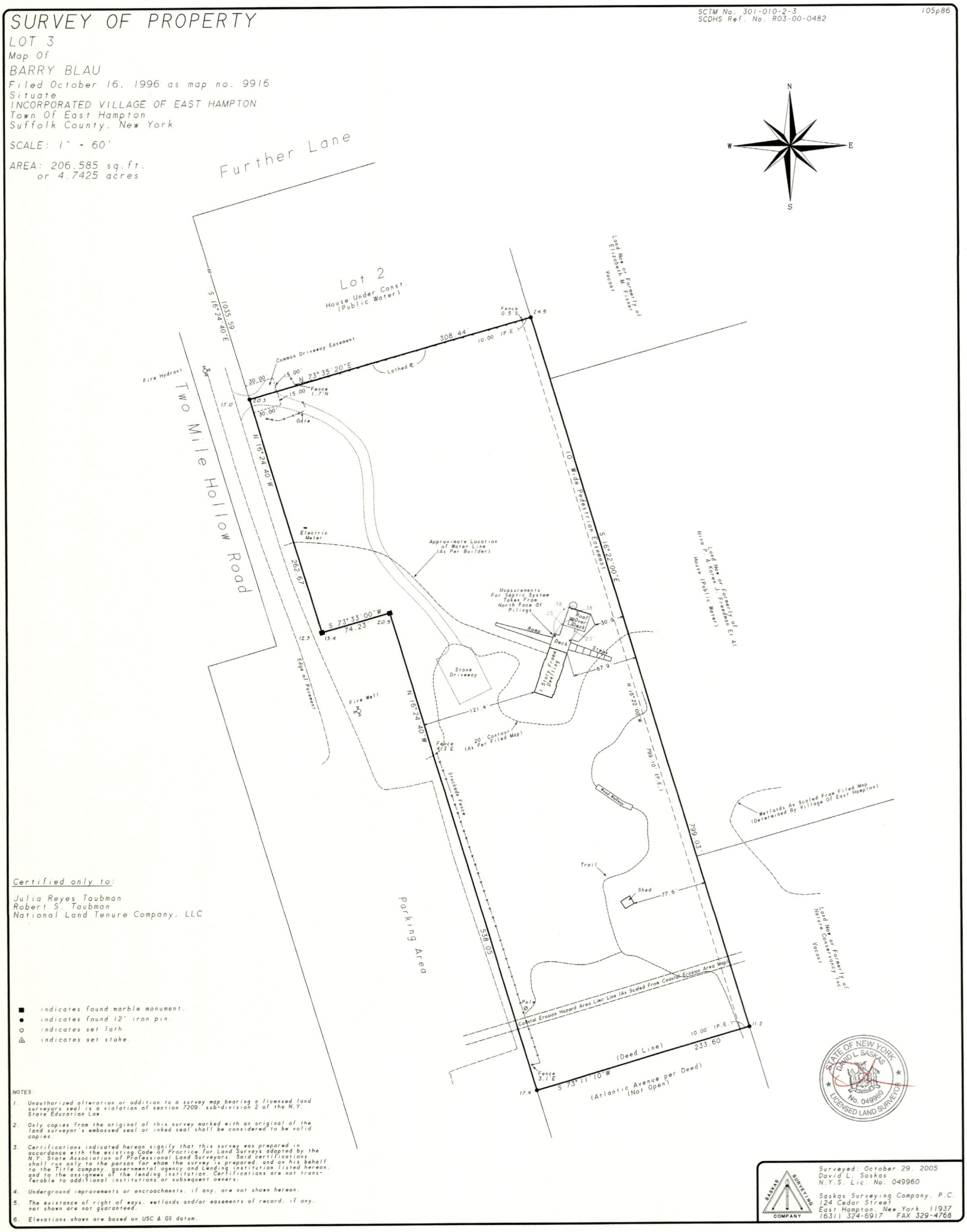
SURVEY OF PROPERTY
LOT 3
Map Of
BARRY BLAU
Filed October 16, 1996 as map no. 9916
Situate
INCORPORATED VILLAGE OF EAST HAMPTON
Town Of East Hampton
Suffolk County, New York
SCALE: 1" = 60'
AREA: 206,585 sq.ft.
or 4.7425 acres
SCTM No. 301-010-2-3
SCDHS Ref. No. R03-00-0482
105p86
N
S
E
W
Further Lane
Two Mile Hollow Road
Lot 2
House Under Const.
(Public Water)
Land Now or Formerly of
Elizabeth M. Fisher
Vacant
Land Now or Formerly of
Nina P. & Karen J. Freedman Et Al
House (Public Water)
Land Now or Formerly of
Nature Conservancy Inc.
Vacant
S 16°24'40"E
1035.59'
N 73°35'20"E
308.44'
Common Driveway Easement
Fire Hydrant
Fence 0.5'S
24.5
10.00' (P.E.)
Lathed
Fence 1.7'N
Gate
Electric Meter
N 16°24'40"W
262.67'
S 73°33'00"W
74.23'
Approximate Location of Water Line (As Per Builder)
10' Wide Pedestrian Easement
S 16°22'00"E
Measurements For Septic System Taken From North Face Of Pilings
Ramp
Deck
Steps
Roof Over Deck
Story Frame Dwelling
Stone Driveway
Edge of Pavement
Fire Well
N 16°24'40"W
121.4'
67.9'
30.9'
20' Contour (As Per Filed Map)
Fence 4.3'E
Stockade Fence
N 16°22'00"W
799.10' (P.E.)
Wood Walkway
Wetlands As Scaled From Filed Map (Determined By Village Of East Hampton)
799.03'
Trail
Shed
77.6'
Parking Area
538.05'
Pole
Coastal Erosion Hazard Area Limit Line (As Scaled From Coastal Erosion Area Map)
10.00' (P.E.)
11.2
(Deed Line)
233.60'
Fence 3.1'E
17.4
S 73°11'10"W
(Atlantic Avenue per Deed)
(Not Open)
Certified only to:
Julia Reyes Taubman
Robert S. Taubman
National Land Tenure Company, LLC
■ indicates found marble monument.
● indicates found 12" iron pin.
○ indicates set lath.
△ indicates set stake.
NOTES:
1. Unauthorized alteration or addition to a survey map bearing a licensed land surveyors seal is a violation of section 7209, sub-division 2 of the N.Y. State Education Law.
2. Only copies from the original of this survey marked with an original of the land surveyor's embossed seal or inked seal shall be considered to be valid copies.
3. Certifications indicated hereon signify that this survey was prepared in accordance with the existing Code of Practice for Land Surveys adopted by the N.Y. State Association of Professional Land Surveyors. Said certifications shall run only to the person for whom the survey is prepared, and on his behalf to the Title company, governmental agency and Lending institution listed hereon, and to the assignees of the lending institution. Certifications are not transferable to additional institutions or subsequent owners.
4. Underground improvements or encroachments, if any, are not shown hereon.
5. The existance of right of ways, wetlands and/or easements of record, if any, not shown are not guaranteed.
6. Elevations shown are based on USC & GS datum.
STATE OF NEW YORK
DAVID L. SASKAS
No. 049960
LICENSED LAND SURVEYOR
SASKAS SURVEYING COMPANY
Surveyed: October 29, 2005
David L. Saskas
N.Y.S. Lic. No. 049960
Saskas Surveying Company, P.C.
124 Cedar Street
East Hampton, New York 11937
(631) 324-6917 FAX 329-4768

FOR A LOVE OF DESIGN

When Julie Reyes Taubman and her husband Bobby Taubman purchased a five-acre parcel of land facing the Atlantic Ocean at the end of Two Mile Hollow Road in East Hampton, New York, in 2005, they knew only one thing about the house that they would build there: they wanted it to look nothing like the traditionally-styled gabled houses covered in shingles which for the last couple of decades had been popping up all over the Hamptons. Those expansive and sumptuous residences witnessed architects moving away from the small, boxy forms of the postwar generation of modern beach houses by seeking refuge in a much earlier past, while giving their clients a degree of grandeur that the modest modern boxes had consciously rejected.

This was not what either Taubman sought. Julie Taubman, a photographer and collector of 20th-century furniture and design, had a discerning eye and a fondness for the unorthodox. She would have preferred to build nothing at all rather than have a house that could be mistaken for another shingled trophy of Wall Street success. It was important to her that her house be memorable for something more than its square footage. In fact, she often said that she did not want a particularly large house, just a special one, one that would demonstrate a new idea in a new way, and not look like something that had been built before. Bobby Taubman, who ran his family's real estate enterprise, the Taubman Companies, had inherited from his father, A. Alfred Taubman, one of the inventors of the modern shopping center, a sense of himself as a businessman and a patron. He understood construction, but at the same time believed that architecture was more than a frill and had seen how paying attention to design had added value to his family's shopping centers. In the late 1970s, Alfred Taubman had purchased a house in Bloomfield Hills, Michigan, designed and built a decade earlier for Lynn Townsend, chairman of American Motors, by Alden B. Dow, one of Frank Lloyd Wright's most prominent disciples. It was the sort of modern

PAGE 32
Survey of Property on Two Mile Hollow Road, produced for Julie Reyes Taubman and Robert S. Taubman by David L. Saskas, Saskas Surveying Company, P. C., East Hampton, New York, October 29, 2005

Alden B. Dow, Lynn A. Townsend Residence, Bloomfield Hills, Michigan, 1963

34

house that could leave no one indifferent to architecture's potential to shape sensibility. Soon afterward, Alfred Taubman would commission the architect Richard Meier to build him a house along the inland waterway in Palm Beach, and after that, a penthouse in New York City.

While Bobby had inherited his father's practical side, he also knew how excited Alfred Taubman, who was trained as an architect, could become when encountering a work of art or architecture that moved him, and had come to share that excitement. Building shopping centers was a way for the elder Taubman, who would eventually come to own Sotheby's auction house, to collect the art he loved, and to house his family in notable works of modern architecture. Still, Bobby was at first hesitant about building a new house, worried that it would take too much time and effort—and he had already negotiated a deal to buy an existing oceanfront house in East Hampton when Julie saw the land at the end of Two Mile Hollow Road.

"I knew that Julie wanted to do a house with a great architect," he said, acknowledging that the new parcel of open land Julie had seen, which was twice the size of the other property, was an unusual opportunity that might not come again. It was not only a lot of acreage, but it was on the most desirable stretch of oceanfront in the Hamptons, the Atlantic Double Dunes, unique in the northeastern United States, where a primary dune and a secondary dune run parallel to one another for two and a half miles. Houses built beside the double dunes face not only the surf and a sandy beach, but also a rich natural dunescape. To show the potential of the land, its first owner had commissioned architect Preston T. Phillips to design a temporary structure, a small white pavilion of wood and glass called The Butterfly House' (2001), oriented to feature the beauty of views across the dunes to the ocean. (p. 77)

Moreover, Bobby understood how excited his wife was at the prospect of building a unique house. And development, after all, was certainly in his DNA. Putting aside his concerns, he agreed to go ahead. Over the years, as the project moved forward, Taubman would appear to vacillate between measured support for the design, practical criticisms of certain aspects of it, and unbridled enthusiasm about the construction adventure he and his wife had embarked on. What never wavered was his belief in Julie's sensibility and commitment to design.

Julie Reyes Taubman, like her husband, grew up in a self-made family with substantial resources. The Reyes family built one of the largest private companies in the United States, a global leader in the production and distribution of food and beverages. Unlike Bobby Taubman, she had not entered her family's business. She pursued her love of 20th-century design with a combination of zeal, connoisseurship, and relentless determination. She collected widely, to the point of acquiring warehouse space near her residence in Michigan when her acquisitions no longer fit easily into her own home. But she bought with discernment, often supporting the work of new young artists or talented designers whose work was off the radar of most other collectors.

Julie was one of the founders of the Museum of Contemporary Art Detroit (MOCAD), and had produced a book of her own photographs, *Detroit: 138 Square Miles*, which was different than almost every coffee table book of contemporary photography in the way it embodied her highly personal sensibility. A gimlet-eyed documentarian, she used her camera to record the deterioration of Detroit in meticulous detail, moving back and forth between the monumental buildings of downtown, the everyday structures of local neighborhoods, and the people who occupy both. And while it was clear that she lamented the state of the city, she never fell into easy nostalgia. She was neither a condescending photographer nor a sentimental one. "If what happened in Detroit is a crime, Julia's book is the crime story," her friend Elmore Leonard wrote in his foreword, and indeed, she saw the sprawling physical city as both perpetrator and victim, a story of both majesty and tragedy—an especially heartbreaking one because to her, it remained majestic in its decline. "We are blessed in Detroit that our streets are not silent," she wrote. "Our town's abandoned factories, train stations, warehouses, and school buildings speak to us in ways that demand our attention and respect. It is a privilege to know this place."

Zago Architects, Museum of Contemporary Art Detroit (MOCAD), Detroit, Michigan, 2006

ABOVE
Eero Saarinen, Dulles International Airport, Chantilly, Virginia, 1958–62

BELOW
Eero Saarinen, TWA Flight Center, John F. Kennedy International Airport, 1959–62

It was no surprise that neither of the Taubmans would want to build a conventional house, and that Julie would see the oceanfront land in East Hampton as the opportunity to commission a building that would push architecture forward in the way that the furniture and objects she most responded to had pushed design forward. She grew up loving the work of Eero Saarinen, which she came to know first through visits to Dulles Airport near her hometown of Washington, D.C., and she would later say that Saarinen's TWA Flight Center at the John F. Kennedy Airport in New York was her favorite building of all. When she moved to Detroit after her marriage to Bobby Taubman, one of the things that most excited her about the city was the presence of the Cranbrook Academy of Art, in nearby Bloomfield Hills whose campus was designed by Eliel Saarinen, Eero's father, and where Eero Saarinen as well as Charles and Ray Eames had studied design. Julie would become an active member of Cranbrook's governing board.

Her love of cutting-edge modern design was, in part, a yearning for the shattering of convention that modernism had once represented. Her beloved Dulles Airport was a daring building in the early 1960s, not just because it was a striking sculptural object, but because Saarinen conceived it as an

Eliel Saarinen, Cranbrook Academy of Art campus, view of the Triton Pools with Carl Milles sculptures, Bloomfield Hills, Michigan, 1926–43

altogether new paradigm for airport design. As a child, Julie recalled, she found it "exhilarating." When she began to collect, she would have little interest in the mid-century modern objects that had become familiar household staples in sophisticated homes and apartments. In other words, she did not so much want an Eames chair as she wanted to find the chair that would startle and excite people now in the way that Charles and Ray Eames's designs had done 70 years ago—or, better still, the chair from 70 years ago that had been too unconventional to become as popular as an Eames and had been relegated unfairly to the sidelines of modern history.

"She wouldn't ever buy something predictable," said Michael Lewis, the interior designer who came to play a major role in the realization of the house that the Taubmans built in East Hampton. "Nothing about her was bourgeois. She was completely bohemian, but with quality –she could wear a couture evening dress with a pair of clogs and carry it off." Another of her close friends, the creative director and collector Dennis Freedman, said "Julie didn't think like everyone else—she challenges the idea of taste." Freedman had assembled a major collection of radical Italian furniture from the 1960s, and Taubman saw herself as having a similar taste for the unorthodox. She had the remarkable combination of a refined eye, a love of history, and a willingness to break free of established norms.

Like her husband, Julie was excited by buildings. It was surely no accident that she selected for the cover of her book a photograph of Albert Kahn's massive, abandoned Packard factory of 1903, one of the first significant

Julie Reyes Taubman, *Detroit, 138 Square Miles* (Detroit: MOCAD, 2011)

modern industrial buildings in Detroit. At the time her book was published, the factory was believed to be the largest empty building in the United States. It sent the clear message that the Detroit which had fallen apart had been a bold city of assertive modernity, a place with nothing genteel about it, a city in which architects, working with committed industrialists, set out to create not just economic might, but the physical form of an exciting new world. Modernist dreams to remake the world may not have succeeded in Detroit, but Julie remained no less excited by them. To both Julie and Bobby Taubman, buildings were full of potential to make life better. They were not static objects so much as things to which a knowledgeable and passionate client working with a skilled architect could give shape and direction. And the best buildings could demonstrate how to change the world.

She loved the long process of design, and her curiosity seemed to have no limits. "She would read every magazine, try everything, see everything, always building her visual dictionary," noted Michael Lewis. For years, she would drop clippings and photographs of houses into folders with labels like 'Inspirations' and 'Interesting Houses'. Her Interesting Houses folder contained images ranging from highly sculptural concrete houses by John Lautner in California to pristine modernist houses by Richard Meier in Florida, houses by Philip Johnson on Long Island, and houses by Jorn Utzon in Denmark. She was especially fond of a group of houses designed by Jacques Couëlle, an artist and self-taught architect associated with the circle of Picasso and Dali in the South of France. Couëlle's approach to architecture evolved in ever closer rapport with nature and landscape, eventually relying on sculptural modeling rather than architectural drawings. Couëlle, who died in 1996, was one of the great 20th-century design iconoclasts of France. In 1926, he was commissioned to design a chateau in Castellaras, on a hilltop overlooking Cannes, where he incorporated

LEFT
John Lautner, Arthur Elrod House, Araby Cove, Palm Springs, California, 1968

RIGHT
John Lautner, Russell and Gina Garcia House, Hollywood Hills, Los Angeles, California, 1962

historicizing architectural details sourced from buildings spanning centuries. In 1950, the abandoned site was bought by a Parisian banker who commissioned Couëlle to design a village of traditional Provencal houses around the chateau. Shortly after that, he designed and built five prototypes for a modernist housing development on an adjacent site slated for development, coining the term "*maison-paysage*" (landscape house) to describe them as they were conceived as organic rather than geometric to accommodate the contours of the site. Those were the houses that captivated Julie.

Julie also clipped an article from *Architectural Digest* called "Living in Modern Monuments," which contained interviews with the owners of houses by Frank Gehry and Mies van der Rohe, among others. The piece carried the subtitle "Five Answers to the Question 'What's it Like to Dwell in a Work of Art?'," which for her was not a rhetorical question at all. It was the very issue she thought about.

UPPER AND LOWER LEFT, LOWER RIGHT
Jacques Couëlle, *maisons-paysages*. Castellaras-le-Neuf, overlooking Cannes at Mouans-Sartoux, Alpes-Maritimes, France, 1962–65

UPPER RIGHT
Jacques Couëlle, Monte Mano, a *maison-paysage* the architect designed for himself, Costa Smeralda, Sardinia, Italy, 1970

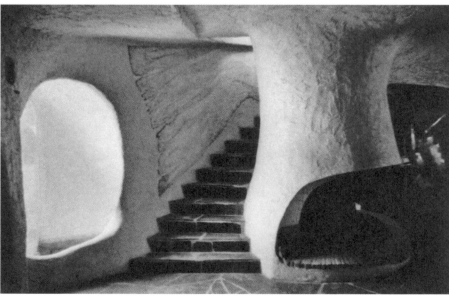

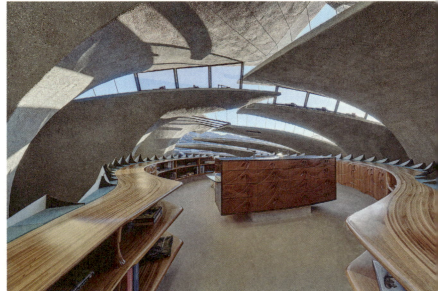

Kendrick Bangs Kellogg, High Desert House, originally the Doolittle House, Joshua Tree, California, 2001

ABOVE
John Randal McDonald, Thunderbird House (originally the Penrith House), Rancho Mirage, California, 1961

BELOW
Kendrick Bangs Kellogg, The Chart House restaurant, Rancho Mirage, California, 1978

In 2006, the year after Julie and Bobby Taubman purchased the land in East Hampton, they acquired an unusual mid-century modern house in the vicinity of the world capital of mid-century modern design, Palm Springs, which Julie redesigned with the help of one friend, designer, writer, and architectural historian Brad Dunning, and furnished with the help of another, Dennis Freedman, whose eye for unusual modern pieces paralleled her own. Not far from the Thunderbird Country Club in Rancho Mirage, itself a mid-century modern landmark, the house designed by John Randal McDonald is a dramatic structure of stone, travertine, glass, and wood whose pointed shape loosely echoes late Frank Lloyd Wright. Julie called it the 'Thunderbird House'. A logo with a thunderbird painted on the roof was repeated on tableware and bathrobes in the house. After the Taubmans had owned the Thunderbird House for several years, but before they had selected an architect for East Hampton, they learned that the High Desert House, a celebrated design by Kendrick Bangs Kellogg completed in 1993 in nearby Joshua Tree, had come on the market. They went to see the house, a remarkable assemblage of curving concrete elements that resembled dinosaur bones arrayed like elegantly crafted vertebrae across the desert rocks. It made John Lautner, to whose work Kellogg's bore some similarity, seem almost tame. Both Taubmans found it "spectacular," Bobby recalled. "When you're in the house you're one with nature." The organic nature of Kellogg's work appealed to Julie. She particularly liked the Chart House restaurant in Rancho Mirage, which like the High Desert House seemed to represent the freedom from convention that had attracted her to Jacques Couëlle. The Taubmans wondered if Kellogg might be an architect they would want to work with someday.

By the time they were ready to select an architect for their oceanfront site in East Hampton, Julie felt prepared to take on what she hoped would be her culminating statement as a collector and patron: the making of a house that would be like no other house. She did not interpret that as meaning a house that would become a model for others, a house that would inspire imitations in the way that Charles Gwathmey's 1965 house for his parents, just a mile further east in Amagansett, had launched a thousand stark, angled beach houses in its wake. The house that Julie envisioned would be one of a kind, the way Kellogg's High Desert House or Jacques Couëlle's group of five houses at Castellaras were. It would not have to be large, but it would be unique, like Frank Lloyd Wright's Fallingwater or Mies van der Rohe's Farnsworth House or Richard Neutra's Lovell House—a house that people would admire and that would have a lasting impact on the culture of architecture. It would, Julie Taubman hoped, give her family relaxing summers beside the Atlantic Ocean, and at the same time embody the passion she felt that the most daring architecture could inspire.

WHERE MODERNISM FLOURISHED

PAGE 56
Phillip Johnson, Farney House, Sagaponack, New York, 1947

More than two decades before Julie and Bobby Taubman bought their oceanfront land, Alfred Taubman had commissioned the architect Jaquelin T. Robertson to renovate an expansive house on the dunes of Southampton, 15 miles to the west, and both Bobby and his family were accustomed to spending vacation time in eastern Long Island. In 1990, Bobby's sister Gayle Kalisman had hired the architect Michael Graves to build a house for her family in Wainscott, a village just west of East Hampton, further testament to the family's interest in commissioning works of serious architecture.

For several years, Bobby and Julie had rented a house in Amagansett, and they knew that although the towns known collectively as 'the Hamptons' had reputations as upscale resorts, the entire area, and East Hampton in particular, had a parallel history as a magnet for artists and architects with a modernist sensibility. If that aspect of the region's history had been overshadowed by the tsunami of affluence that had pushed through the Hamptons in recent decades, East Hampton's connections to postwar abstract expressionism were nevertheless an appealing part of its identity for the Taubmans. And these were not casual connections at all: Jackson Pollack had lived in Springs, a wooded section of town north of East Hampton village, and did much of his most important work in his small shingled studio beside Accobonac Creek until he died in a drunk-driving accident in 1956. Willem de Kooning, who moved to East Hampton from New York in 1963, lived not far from Pollock's house until his death in 1997. Numerous other artists, including Robert Motherwell, Max Ernst, Adolph Gottlieb, Saul Steinberg, Esteban Vicente, and the sculptor Costantino Nivola, found East Hampton and Amagansett appealing both as a refuge from New York and as an environment in which to pursue creative work. Roy Lichtenstein and Larry Rivers lived in nearby Southampton. All of them

Le Corbusier painting a mural on an interior wall of the Cnstantno Nivola cottage in The Springs, East Hampton, New York, 1950

were the heirs to a Hamptons artistic tradition that went all the way back to artists like Winslow Homer, Childe Hassam, William Merritt Chase, Edwin Austin Abbey, and Thomas Moran.

The area had a second history—somewhat less well known—of enthusiasm for modern architecture which only occasionally overlapped with its role as a haven for modern painters. Motherwell, one of the first modern artists to come to East Hampton, commissioned the French modernist Pierre Chareau to design a weekend home and studio for him in 1946, which Chareau crafted out of a pair of Quonset huts, an even more determined attempt to establish a connection between modern architecture and factory-made industrial design than the celebrated house Charles and Ray Eames would build for themselves three years later in Pacific Palisades, California. An ambitious modernist statement of a very different sort was the estate of the artist Alfonso Ossorio, The Creeks, a sprawling property on Georgica Pond in East Hampton. The estate designed by Grosvenor Atterbury c.1899, which Ossorio reconceived into what the writer Alastair Gordon has called "a surrealist theme park," turned Atterbury's staid architecture into an intense and hyperactive essay of modernist juxtaposition.

But places like Motherwell's and Ossorio's, where the ambitions of architecture and modern art coincided, were the exceptions. Most of the modern artists who settled in East Hampton had limited means and lived in traditional farmhouses, like Pollack and his wife, the artist Lee Krasner, and Costantino Nivola and his wife Ruth, who also lived and worked in Springs. When the Nivolas hosted Le Corbusier for the weekend in 1950, the architect told them he found their house attractive, but felt that it needed a mural, and proceeded to paint not one, but two of them on their living room walls.

LEFT
Pierre Chareau, House and studio for Robert Motherwell, East Hampton, New York, 1946, with 1956 alterations

RIGHT
Grosvenor Atterbury, The Creeks, designed for Albert and Adele Herter, Georgica Pond, East Hampton, New York, 1899; purchased in 1951 by the artist Alfonso Ossorio and transformed to include a sculpture park, and a conifer arboretum

Where modernism flourished

Most of the grander architecture in the Hamptons, houses occupied by the wealthy who saw eastern Long Island as a resort, not as a place of artistic inspiration, were traditional in style. But here and there, glimmers of modernism pushed their way through in a few remarkable instances even before the modern artists came to East Hampton after World War II. The architect William Muschenheim designed a group of International Style bath houses for his family's compound in Hampton Bays in 1930, and a year later, the financier Lucien Hamilton Tyng put up The Shallows in Southampton, an expansive villa of white stucco designed by Peabody, Wilson & Brown. Then came the Sandbox, a boxy wooden house designed by Frances Breese Miller with Lansing Holden, built in 1933 on the dunes in Bridgehampton. A few years later, in 1937, East Hampton got its first International Style house, a villa for Myrtle Shepherd by G. Piers Brookfield.

Still, the story of modern architecture in the Hamptons before World War II is a short one. Other than a large beach house overlooking the ocean on the cliffs of Montauk Point designed by Antonin Raymond, a colleague and protégé of Frank Lloyd Wright, it mainly consisted of a few examples of work in the International Style by architects who otherwise had no notable impact on architecture of the time. None of these first, early efforts at bringing modernism to the Hamptons yielded a building of great architectural significance, though every one of them was an earnest work by a client or an architect who felt the stirrings of a new style and wanted to give expression to these feelings far more than they wanted to conform to the established architectural order of the day. This was particularly true of Frances Breese Miller, who had grown up at The Orchard, her family's estate in Southampton designed by Stanford White c.1895–1906. She saw her starkly modern house, which she designed largely by herself, as a statement of rejection of the milieu in which she had been raised, and as a setting that would encourage a simple life by the sea.

LEFT
William Muschenheim, Bath houses on the dunes, Hampton Bays, Southampton, New York, 1931

RIGHT
Antonin Raymond, Interior view of the Charles Briggs and Raoul Carrera House, Old Montauk Highway, Montauk, New York, 1941–42

TOP TO BOTTOM
Frances Breese Miller with Lansing Holden, The Sandbox, Bridgehampton, New York, 1933

Peabody, Wilson & Brown, The Shallows, Southhampton, New York, 1931

Antonin Raymond, Charles Briggs and Raoul Carrera House, Old Montauk Highway, Montauk, New York, 1941–42

61   Where modernism flourished

Miller's house was exceptionally prescient, since after the war, as modern artists began to arrive, numerous architects came to eastern Long Island and set out to design houses very much like the Sandbox—wooden boxes that were intended as celebrations of simple, unpretentious leisure. What was notable about the houses that Peter Blake, Robert Rosenberg, Andrew Geller, George Nelson, Percival Goodman, Paul Lester Wiener, Alexander Knox, Philip Johnson, and others designed in the Hamptons in the 1950s and 1960s was not just their simple, even stark shapes and their openness to the outdoors, but their modesty in comparison with the villas of another era. Lucien Tyng's house was a grand villa of 24 rooms with a dining room that could seat 30. Only its stylistic garb set it apart from the enormous Shingle Style mansions that were its neighbors in Southampton. But houses like Tyng's represented a way of living that seemed to have little relevance in the 1950s, and as younger professional families began to see the Hamptons as a place for casual weekend escape, they sought easy, relaxed houses, not mansions but small houses that were conceived to be run without staff. Modern architecture became a way to express a new form of middle-class leisure. In this sense, Hamptons modern was at once radical and understated.

The houses of the first postwar generation of modernism in the Hamptons were relatively simple pavilions on the dunes, in the woods, or on open lawns—in each case closely connected to the outdoors. They represented another world entirely from the estates hidden behind privets and high gates that filled most of the established village centers of Southampton and East Hampton. The clients who built these new houses were not the gentry, but young sophisticated professionals, people who, like Frances Breese

BELOW LEFT
Paul Lester Weiner, Robert Scull House, East Hampton, New York, 1962

BELOW RIGHT
Andrew Geller, Double Diamond House, Westhampton Beach, New York, 1959

Miller, wanted this new architecture to express the open, casual life they sought. Their houses were almost always built simply and inexpensively, and in many instances were designed only for summer, not year-round use. Philip Johnson's first commission as an architect, completed in 1946 (three years before he finished his iconic Glass House in New Canaan, Connecticut), was a boxy wooden structure designed for Eugene Farney on the ocean in Sagaponack, a farming community between East Hampton and Bridgehampton (p. 56). Johnson based the design on an unbuilt house by Mies van der Rohe for the Resor family in Jackson Hole, Wyoming. The Farney House consisted of two wood-enclosed sections separated by a deck and breezeway, sleek and neatly balanced between openness and enclosure, all appearing to float above the Sagaponack dunes.

Peter Blake's Pinwheel House in Water Mill, just east of Southampton, which he built for his family in a potato field in 1954, was simpler still, but more ingenious: a wooden box, 24 feet square, raised four feet above the ground, with four solid walls that rolled on tracks like enormous barn doors, creating the impression of a pinwheel when they were all slid open. The box contained one large open living space, with two tiny bedrooms and a bath tucked below. When the sliding walls were opened, the house connected on every side with the field around it; when they were closed, it was a tight box, fully protected from the weather. It was a house with four facades: an abstract object in the field, playing off against nature and in every way distinct from it. Blake's house owed a certain debt to a house completed two years earlier by Paul Rudolph, the Walker Guest House in Florida, but Blake had boiled the idea of a structure that could alternate between open pavilion and closed box down to an even simpler, purer essence.

Peter Blake, The Pinwheel House, Water Mill, Southampton, New York, 1954, with Blake sliding a panel into place

Through the 1950s, there were more and more notable houses, and if none rose to the iconic level of Mies van der Rohe's Farnsworth House, Richard Neutra's houses in Los Angeles, or Paul Rudolph's early work in Florida, not to mention those of Frank Lloyd Wright, who never in his long and prolific career built a house in the Hamptons, the first postwar modern houses of the Hamptons did collectively constitute a significant body of work. In those years, the work was too varied to be called a 'style', and it included such buildings as Alexander Knox's playful, origami-like round pavilion beside Mecox Bay in Bridgehampton; George Nelson and Gordon Chadwick's striking Spaeth House in East Hampton, a re-interpretation in modernist terms of a classic Stanford White house; and Robert Rosenberg's glass box beside Two Mile Hollow Beach in East Hampton, just to the west of the land that Julie and Robert Taubman would buy decades later—a house that Philip Johnson would call a poor man's version of his own Glass House. What joined these different houses together was their shared commitment to leisure, simplicity, and the avant-garde. Probably nowhere else in the United States did a body of postwar architecture bring these often-conflicting goals together as effectively as it did in the Hamptons.

Because these three impulses, leisure, simplicity, and the avant-garde, were not really the same, and however tightly they may have been intertwined in these modernist houses, a conflict simmered beneath the surface. The importance of leisure bespoke a yearning for the resort life, which suggested that these were in many ways a middle-class version of the older, grander Hamptons estates, stripped of their grandiosity, but every bit as committed to relaxation as a goal. Could this truly be avant-garde? It was one thing to be an artist like Pollack, zealously and intensely painting powerful

ABOVE
Alexander Knox, Mecox Bay House, Bridgehampton, New York, 1959

BELOW LEFT
George Nelson and Gordon Chadwick, Otto Spaeth House, East Hampton, New York, 1956

BELOW RIGHT
Robert Rosenberg, Two Mile Hollow Beach House, East Hampton, New York, 1952

pictures in a barn; was it as radical to be sipping cocktails in a wood and glass box? Was architecture really challenging bourgeois norms only in the name of relaxation?

There were some architects who favored things other than the pared-down sleekness of a modernist seaside pavilion, but they were not building actively in the Hamptons. Some, like the theorist and visionary architect Frederick Kiesler, were barely building at all. In the summer of 1960, Kiesler rented a cottage not far from that of his friend Costantino Nivola in Amagansett, and a studio in nearby Springs, where he worked until his death in 1965. Having long been more a part of the art world than the architecture community, Kiesler represented a determined avant-garde sensibility. He had designed Peggy Guggenheim's legendary Gallery of the Twentieth Century in New York in 1942, with sensuous, curving walls that he hoped would evoke the spirit of surrealism, a design that was the utter opposite of the crisp lines of the International Style. Kiesler's best-known design, an unbuilt project he called the *Endless House* dating from c.1950, which the critic Jason Farago would describe as "a womblike void whose ceiling folds into the walls," was not designed for the Hamptons or any actual site at all, but its image, looking as much like a living being as a piece of construction, would fascinate architects, including Ricardo Scofidio, Elizabeth Diller, and Charles Renfro. When Diller, Scofidio, and Renfro came to design the Taubman house more than half century after Kiesler, and sought through it to revive the spirit of the avant-garde at the eastern end of Long Island, their design would call Kiesler's *Endless House* to mind.

BELOW LEFT AND RIGHT
Frederick Kiesler, Two interior views of the *Endless House* model, 1959

It was not a surrealist like Kiesler, but a pair of younger modernists, Charles Gwathmey and Richard Meier, who would make the strongest architectural mark on the Hamptons in the 1960s, building on the work of their predecessors by struggling to make more complex forms that they hoped would push modernist architecture forward. They had no interest in simplifying and paring down: the purity of the glass box had lost its allure, and they wanted to dig deeper into modernism, as if to psychoanalyze it by breaking its shapes apart and putting them back together again into newly composed, more intricate wholes. If their work was a bit self-conscious, it was also ambitious, and visually compelling. And if the program was still a weekend house for leisure, these houses did not recede as neutral backdrops the way many of their predecessors did.

They were still far from lavish. Gwathmey's celebrated house and studio for his parents in Amagansett, completed in 1965, cost only $35,000 to build—cheap, indeed, for a structure that would come to have such an iconic presence in 20th-century American architecture. But it was not a plain box any more than Meier's Saltzman House in East Hampton, completed in 1969 and heavily influenced by Le Corbusier's Villa Savoye, was a plain box. Gwathmey was all diagonals, pushing through space and poking up the roofline. The house was a simple structure that he managed to contort into a highly active sculptural form, even more so when he added a studio for his father, the painter Robert Gwathmey, a smaller version of the main house, and the two buildings became sculptural pieces playing off one another in space.

ABOVE
Charles Gwathmey, Gwathmey Studio and Residence, Amagansett, New York, 1965

BELOW
Richard Meier, Renny and Ellin Saltzman House, East Hampton, New York, 1969

The Gwathmey house inspired countless imitations, few if any of which possessed its simple, blunt self-assurance. Ordinary, even banal as many of these wood and glass structures with their vertical cedar siding and stark, angled rooflines were, they did constitute a certain critical mass. Before long, enough houses in this genre had been built to constitute

a modern vernacular for East Hampton, Amagansett, Bridgehampton, and the other villages of the Hamptons—a general style of the time that created the sense of a whole that was more than the sum of its parts, the way the old, shingled houses of another era had become a vernacular three-quarters of a century earlier.

As this style became more widespread, it seemed to lose what radical edge the earlier modernist work had. If modernist architecture in the Hamptons had begun as a radical response to the stolid and tired forms of architectural history, by the mid-1960s it had become a style of middle-class aspiration, more than anything else. And if this was true of architects like Meier and Gwathmey and the many who followed them, it was equally true of Norman Jaffe, a gifted architect who based his practice in Bridgehampton and tried to craft a more localized version of modernism, vaguely influenced by the horizontal lines and use of wood and stone characteristic of Frank Lloyd Wright, but at the same time highly original.

The assertive, abstract sculptural shapes on the dunes and the potato fields of the Hamptons were so common by the 1970s—one article referred to Amagansett as "Arrogancet"—that a reaction was inevitable, and it came in the form of postmodernism, a turning back toward the very historical forms that modernist architects had rejected. A few, like Robert A. M. Stern and Jaquelin Robertson, influenced by the writings and designs of Robert Venturi, began to incorporate allusions to traditional architecture in several houses in the Hamptons that were in other ways modern and original buildings. So, too, with the house Michael Graves designed for Bobby Taubman's sister Gayle Kalisman and her husband, one of the most ambitious essays in postmodernism ever built in the Hamptons. But by the late 1980s, the edginess of postmodernism began to fade, and new houses in the Hamptons began to resemble the houses of the past more and more literally. Why build a quirky modern twist on a traditional house, the logic went, when you

Norman Jaffe House, Bridgehampton, New York, 1971

could just do a traditional house 'straight'? Making the new look like the old, the very thing that modernists disparaged, became the goal of many architects. And the notion that architecture could be an original art seemed to go by the wayside.

It was not, of course, the first time such a recoiling from the new had happened, and as history shows, this reaction did not necessarily bring bad architecture in its wake. The reality was not so simple. Just as the 1920s and 1930s were decades in which many of the greatest masterpieces of modern architecture were produced, at the same time, they were decades in which some of the finest architecture in traditional styles was created. The turn backwards toward the end of 20th century yielded plenty of fine, even distinguished houses, in the Hamptons as in so many places around the world. The willingness to admit that the grand Shingle Style mansions of East Hampton and Southampton built around the turn of the previous century were not stuffy and obsolete objects, but beautiful works of architecture with a deep connection to place, and as a group constituted a meaningful local vernacular: this was a welcome corrective to what was often a willful blindness to history on the part of the early modernists. One might even go further and acknowledge that turning to historical examples, embracing gables and shingles and porches at that point might be considered a necessary and certainly an understandable response to the excesses of the 1970s, when modernist buildings were plunked down like pieces of sculpture, with little attention to placemaking and little thought about what they would mean when their clashing shapes collided on the dunes. With a view to some of these garish assemblages of anxious angles, it is not surprising that many architects preferred to look to old East Hampton streets like Lily Pond Lane as models.

But—and it is an important 'but'—if modern abstraction had been taken to excess, so was the reaction against it, and it did not take many years before the new Shingle Style houses, their gambrel roofs churned out by developers as if from an assembly line, were the norm. They quickly became another vernacular, another standardized language, but this one a glib, easy way for the new to give itself the air of the venerable. And the houses not only became more traditional, they became bigger and bigger, and one of the most important aspects of postwar Hamptons modernism, its essential plainness and simplicity, was rejected entirely by architects and developers for whom the ideal was not a 1,000-square-foot pavilion on the beach, but a McMansion.

ABOVE
'Home, Sweet Home', British Colonial wood shingled house, East Hampton, New York, c.1750

BELOW
Joel Barkley, Ike, Kligerman & Barkley, Southampton Beach House, New York, 2014

Architecture always expresses not only the cultural impulses of a time, but also the means available to it, and as more and more wealth came to the Hamptons, houses continued to expand. In time, which is to say by the early 2000s, the fashion for replicas of the great shingled houses of old began to fade, like many trends a victim, in part, of overexposure. Modernism began a modest but clear resurgence. History never repeats itself precisely, and most of the modern houses of the Hamptons that were built in the new millennium were not like their predecessors: they had even less of a radical edge, and they shared with their shingled neighbors a tendency toward grandiosity. Modernism in the 2000s usually meant neither modesty nor anything remotely avant-garde, but rather sumptuous villas by architectural firms like Bates Masi, Sawyer Berson, Stelle Lomont Rouhani, and Bohlin Cywinski Jackson, often exquisitely detailed and magnificently crafted.

Where modernism flourished

This generation of houses was, at least symbolically, the descendant of East Hampton houses like Charles Gwathmey's Cogan House of 1971 and his De Menil house of 1979, two early attempts to merge the architect's intense formalist explorations with a grander, more expansive program. A couple of decades later, this was what many more architects were doing, with results that were often elegant and serene, even beautiful. But at the same time, they suggested that modernist architecture had itself taken on many of the qualities of the historical styles it originally set out to supplant: grandeur, sumptuousness, and an association with luxury and refinement. It was a striking paradox that so many of the modernist houses built in the first decades of the 21st century in the Hamptons, by using the modernist vocabulary to express lavishness more than anything new, could almost be said to have connoted a certain conservatism. They were beautiful, but in no way radical—they were houses that were about elegance, not about changing how people viewed the world, or about changing how architecture was made.

Changing how architecture was made, however, was exactly what Julie Taubman sought. She wanted something new and different far more than she wanted something overwhelmingly grand. To recapture the energy of early modernism, to feel the excitement of being on the cutting edge was what she wanted most of all. That was the true heritage of the modernist movement, she believed: to make things that were different, and that would challenge conventional perceptions. And it was with this in mind that she and her husband began their search for an architect.

LEFT
Charles Gwathmey, Gwathmey, Siegel & Associates, Cogan House, East Hampton, New York, 1971

RIGHT
Charles Gwathmey, Gwathmey, Siegel & Associates, De Menil House, East Hampton, New York, 1983

THE QUESTION OF AN ARCHITECT

The Taubmans doubted that a well-established architect would give them the new kind of house they aspired to create; at the same time, they were hesitant to entrust a large commission to someone without at least some degree of experience. They looked at architects from all over the world, and while they were familiar with most practitioners, they asked numerous friends in the academic and design worlds to give them suggestions. Lists begat more lists, and the Taubmans read books, visited houses, and eventually interviewed 22 different architects, almost all of whom were eager for the commission. "To do a house on the dunes like this is a dream for any architect," Bobby Taubman said later. "They all wanted to do it."

They briefly considered Kendrick Bangs Kellogg, the eccentric West Coast architect whose High Desert House in Joshua Tree had so inspired them. But Kellogg worked alone, without the infrastructure of an architecture firm behind him, and had only completed a handful of projects recently, each of which had taken years. He was brilliantly creative, they thought, but he was more of an artist than an architect, and they did not have the confidence that he could execute the house they hoped to build.

Eventually, their research narrowed their preferences to three: Shigeru Ban, the Japanese architect particularly known for his innovative work with paper tubes, which he sometimes used as a construction material; Thomas Phifer, an architect of elegant glass buildings who had worked for Richard Meier for many years and had overseen several of Meier's well-known projects; and Tod Williams and Billie Tsien, partners who were known for their intellectually rigorous, somewhat hard-edged modernism. In 2006, the Taubmans decided to turn the selection process into a small competition and offered the architects funds to produce a simple model that would demonstrate their concept for the house.

Ban, who would later design the delicate, latticework-like Aspen Art Museum, completed in 2014, and the same year be awarded the Pritzker Prize, produced an elegant design that was set over a body of water, with a master bedroom poised atop a waterfall, and children's and guest rooms set below an artificial pond on the roof. It was elaborate—the model included what looked like a museum-scale Calder stabile as a sculpture in the entry court—and absolutely striking, but it seemed, Bobby Taubman felt, "more suited to a house in the tropics. The design was truly remarkable, the master bedroom looked like it was floating in a pond, but we wondered how it would feel in the winter." Julie was so excited about it that she wanted to have Ban develop the design further. Brad Dunning, who had worked with her on the

Thunderbird house, remembered that "she was dazzled and fascinated by it." But cost and impracticality ultimately ruled Ban out. As for Tod Williams and Billie Tsien, who a decade later would be selected to design the Obama Presidential Center, while the Taubmans respected them and felt their work was of the highest quality, their ideas for the house seemed to Julie more restrained and perhaps less daring than she wanted.

That left Phifer, who had proposed a set of separate structures for entertaining and family living, all connected by glass-enclosed links. "It was amazing, it was great, and it solved our program," Bobby Taubman said. They hired Phifer, who began to turn his concept into a final design, and they also contacted Ed Bulgin, whose Southampton contracting firm, Bulgin & Associates, had built many of the most elaborate houses in the area, and who prided himself on his ability to work with different, sometimes untested architectural ideas.

As Phifer and Julie Taubman refined his original proposal into a fully developed design, Julie had some concerns that the process was making the house larger and grander than she had wanted it to be. She worried that Phifer's architecture, beautiful as it was, would not make the radical statement she had in her mind—that it would not look sufficiently different from anything that had been built before. She had always felt that modern elegance by itself was not enough, and indeed, that a house which was too elegant could also feel, by the very fact of its tasteful stylishness, a bit too conservative, especially in the 21st century. To truly be on the cutting edge, Julie Taubman felt, you had to be ready to take the next leap beyond

Thomas Phifer, Original competition scheme, 2007

Thomas Phifer and Partners,
Second design scheme, 2007

ABOVE
Rear elevation

BELOW
Waterfront elevation

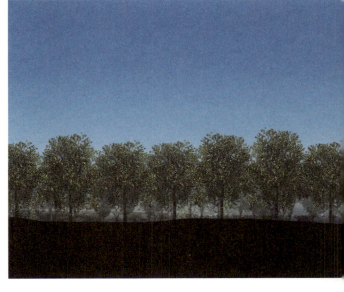

Thomas Phifer and Partners,
First design scheme in final stage
of development, 2007

ABOVE
East elevation

CENTER
South elevation

BELOW
North elevation

The question of an architect

an architecture that could be viewed as a refinement of the International Style modernist vocabulary of the 20th century. The sumptuous modernist villas that were going up in the villages of the Hamptons may not have been backward looking like the shingled mansions that preceded them in the parade of architectural trends, but that hardly made them avant-garde.

Still, Phifer's design, primarily of glass and steel, was hardly a typical Hamptons modern house of the mid-2000s; indeed, no one else was building anything quite like it. Phifer's design was both expansive and minimalist, and its three glass and steel pavilions, for all their size, could also be described as austere. Its elegance and finesse were beyond question, but minimalism was not a quality that Julie Taubman had sought. For more than three years, Phifer and the Taubmans worked on the design, meeting either in Michigan or in Phifer's office in lower Manhattan, as Julie alternated between periods of enthusiasm and periods of doubt. Although their relationship was always cordial and respectful, Phifer felt that he and Julie Taubman had not connected as closely as he wanted his clients to connect, and he came to feel, as he would say later, "that the project was fraught." At one point the Taubmans asked Bill Massie, then architect in residence at Cranbrook in Michigan and an old friend, to advise Phifer in the hope that he might help the architect connect more closely with Julie's ambitions. But the immaculate quality of Phifer's architecture was never the right match for Julie's taste, her friend Dennis Freedman remembered thinking. He recalled that she had expressed doubts to him about whether Phifer could ever create the house she envisioned. Still, the work went on, and in 2008 the Taubmans signed off on the design. Phifer produced a full complement of construction drawings and a contract was negotiated with Ed Bulgin, who arranged for building permits and scheduled a date to start construction.

The bulldozers were poised at Two Mile Hollow Road and ready to start digging the foundation when Julie Taubman called Bulgin. She did not want to go forward with the house, she said. She hoped he would not be too upset, but she had too many doubts about whether the design was exactly what she wanted, despite all the meetings and discussions she and Bobby had with Phifer. Something did not feel right, and she needed to rethink it.

Bobby Taubman was on a business trip in Asia, and although he was startled and unhappy with the abruptness of Julie's decision, when the great financial crisis of 2008 took hold two months later, he came to view her decision as a welcome pause. Perhaps this was not the ideal time to build an ambitious and expensive house, he thought. He hoped that things would come back together again after some time for reflection, and told Tom Phifer that in view of the recession, he and his wife had decided to wait a bit before getting started.

In the meantime, Phifer knew that Julie wasn't fully comfortable with his design, and he decided to use this interim period to produce an entirely different design, one that might respond more directly to Julie's interest in more sculptural form. "I think she really wanted something more like Zaha Hadid," he said. And he devised a new scheme, different from anything he had ever produced, a design that consisted of five separate vaulted forms of different sizes and proportions, as if the Sydney Opera House had been deconstructed and its sections arrayed along the dune like a collection of seashells.

It was certainly sculptural, and it bore a certain resemblance to the Kendrick Kellogg house that Julie found so appealing. But the Taubmans were not sure that Phifer's second scheme was what they wanted either. It was so different from all of the architect's other work that they were not, at first, sure what to make of it. And for all the assertiveness of its shape, it was no more modest than his first design. Julie had not given up on her hope that she could have a house that would somehow manage to echo the understatement as well as the radical sensibility of the earliest modern houses in the Hamptons. The new design, like Phifer's earlier one, could still be described as both monumental and minimalist, but this time with curving instead of straight lines. Phifer would come to prefer it to his original scheme, which he felt had been altered significantly over the lengthy design process; this new scheme, he believed, was more purely his own. But the Taubmans decided not to move forward with this one either, and Bobby Taubman made another call to Phifer, this time to tell him that he and his wife had decided to look for another architect. For Phifer, it was a double loss: first, he felt that his design had been compromised by the many changes he had been asked to make, and then he lost the commission altogether.

Brad Dunning, who remained a close advisor to Julie, even helping to make improvements to the modest Butterfly House by Preston Phillips designed for the previous owner of the property on Two Mile Hollow Road, was not surprised that Julie had decided she could not move forward with Phifer.

Preston T. Phillips, The Butterfly House, East Hampton, New York, 2001

Peter L. Gluck, Gluck+, Project for House in the Dunes, 2009

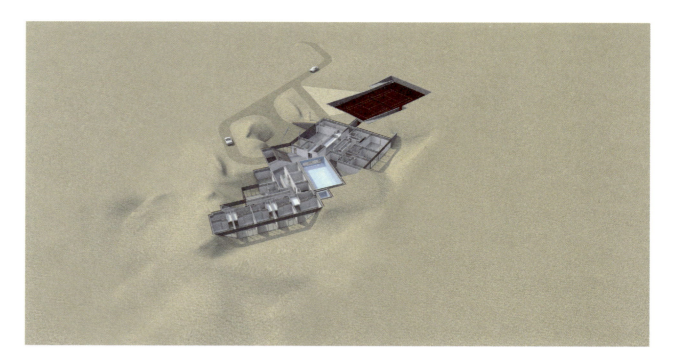

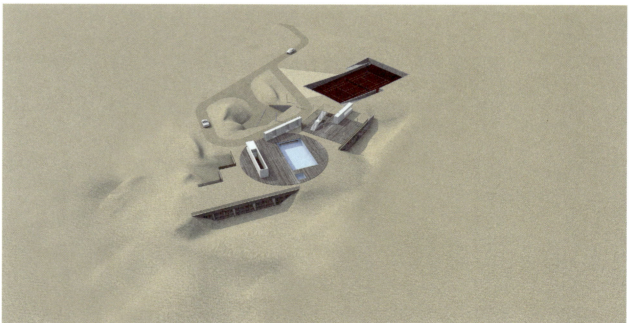

Peter L. Gluck, Gluck+, Project
for House in the Dunes, 2009

TOP TO BOTTOM
Dunes level
Pool level
Upper box level

Julie had heard about Peter Gluck, a talented architect of modernist houses whose firm, Gluck+, specialized in 'design-build', a system by which the architect agreed to produce both the design and the finished house for a specified price. She thought this might be a good way to keep the project on a more modest footing, and toward the end of 2008, the Taubmans began to work with him. Gluck produced a scheme of multiple angular, geometric wood and glass structures, elevated on columns above the dunes and reached by a large staircase, which in some ways seemed like a significantly expanded version of the casual wooden beach houses of a previous Hamptons generation, including those Gluck himself designed in the 1960s. It was surely more sculptural than Phifer's first design, but it was neither particularly modest nor did it have the sophistication of either of Phifer's coolly elegant schemes. By the beginning of 2010, the Taubmans had concluded that Gluck, like Phifer, was not the architect they had been looking for.

By then, six years had passed since they purchased the site in East Hampton, and there was still not a house. There was not even an architect. Julie confided her frustrations to Dennis Freedman, whose collection of radical Italian design she had long admired and who had given her advice about furniture when she was renovating the Thunderbird House in Rancho Mirage, but also while the Taubmans were working on the Phifer design.

Freedman had an idea. "I knew that Bobby's mind was practical, and Julie's mind worked in a different way," he said. "I told Julie that there was only one architecture firm that could do something that she would like, that Bobby would feel was buildable, that could bridge the two of them and satisfy both of them, and that was Diller Scofidio + Renfro."

Peter L. Gluck, Rosenberg Beach House, Sagaponack, New York, 1967

STARTING OVER

In 2010, when Dennis Freedman suggested that the Taubmans interview Diller Scofidio + Renfro, the firm was well on its way to transitioning from its beginnings as a largely experimental studio to being a large, full-service architectural firm. Elizabeth Diller and Ricardo Scofidio founded the Diller + Scofidio studio in 1979. Diller had been a brilliant, highly ambitious student of Scofidio's at The Cooper Union in New York; the two eventually became partners in life as well as work, and married eight years after founding their office. Diller + Scofidio's early years brought it much acclaim in academic circles, as well as the MacArthur 'genius grant' 1999, in recognition of what the foundation called "an alternative form of architectural practice that unites design, performance, and electronic media with cultural and architectural theory and criticism." which seemed like a way of saying that Diller + Scofidio, was more interested in exploring the relationship between architectural space, culture, and politics than in actually designing buildings.

That was not, in fact, the case. For all that its conceptual work and art installations were admired (they were, for example, the focus of a retrospective exhibition at the Whitney Museum in 2003 entitled *Scanning: Aberrant Architectures of Diller + Scofidio*), the two original partners along with Charles Renfro—a Texan who joined the office in 1997 and was added to the firm's name in 2004 when he became a partner—were interested in expanding the studio's range to do more buildings for clients. While they had a handful of completed buildings to their credit, including an apartment building in Gifu, Japan, and a redesign of The Brasserie in the Seagram Building, they had few invitations to build. That had begun to change in 2002, when they were hired to oversee the renovation of the Lincoln Center cultural campus in Midtown Manhattan, and shortly afterward received their first commission for a new, freestanding building, the Institute for Contemporary Art (ICA) in Boston. And soon came the call to design the High Line, the linear park atop an abandoned elevated freight line in New York. The High Line would be a stunning success with both the public and architectural critics, and by the time its first section opened in June 2009, Diller Scofidio + Renfro had become known as one of the leading firms in the country, if not the world, for cultural and institutional projects—the architects to call if you wanted a building that would be on the cutting edge, would get noticed, and yet would still fulfill a complex set of practical demands.

The firm had moved with astonishing speed from its radical beginnings to being architects of choice for large institutions. There were two major commissions from Columbia University and invitations to design The Broad in Los Angeles and the University of California Berkeley Art Museum and Pacific Film Archive. The Shed at Hudson Yards soon followed, a new cultural center based on a conceptual idea of the studio that was incorporated into an immense private real estate development in which DS+R also ended up as co-designers of a condominium tower.

All of this work meant that the career stage that usually establishes the reputation of architects of a highly creative bent, designing private houses or apartments for sophisticated clients, barely happened for the firm. There was the Kinney (Plywood) House in Briarcliff, New York, in 1980, and in 1981, the architects designed the *Slow House* in North Haven on Long Island Sound for an art collector, for which construction was started in 1990 but never completed, owing to the collapse of the art market at the same time. The house was to have been funded by the sale of two Cy Twombly drawings; in the end, the drawings and models for the *Slow House* were acquired for the Museum of Modern Art's permanent collection. Still, these were relatively modest houses, since for years, the studio had been too small and too marginal to attract clients such as the Taubmans. And then, suddenly, DS+R were too big and its partners too busy flying around the world designing museums and concert halls to take on individual houses for private clients.

Dennis Freedman was not concerned about this: the Taubmans were not ordinary clients, and he thought that if DS+R could be persuaded to make time to design any house, it should be this one. He reminded the Taubmans that the ICA in Boston had been well received, and he was sure that the firm could respond to the Taubmans' vision and would be able to manage a project of the size they had in mind. Nevertheless, Bobby Taubman was worried. "DS+R has never built a house," he said to Freedman, exaggerating only slightly. Freedman offered to join the Taubmans for a preliminary meeting with the partners of the firm.

"Bobby and Julie were clear about wanting this to be their house, not a DS+R house," Freedman said. But it was not entirely clear what a DS+R house would actually look like, given how conceptual most of their earlier residential projects had been. The *Slow House*, designed for a site not far from East Hampton, for example, which Liz Diller would later describe as "a decelerating curve that grew in height and progressively leaned as it expanded," could also be thought of as an investigation into the relationship of idyllic views to daily life, with video cameras creating recordings of the

Diller + Scofidio, *Slow House*, conceptual model for a weekend house that reveals a transition from the entryway, a single door, to an expansive picture window framing views of the surroundings on Long Island Sound, New York, 1991

Starting over

ocean view that could be played back at night or in stormy weather—an expression of an idea as much as an exercise in creating physical form. There was somewhat more formal definition to the firm's *Phantom House*. Designed in 2007 and envisioned for a desert location in the southwest, it consisted of a small, climate-controlled glass box juxtaposed with several exterior living spaces set above, below, and beside it. The intricately interlocking pattern of indoor and outdoor spaces was intended to encourage maximum outdoor living and minimize the need for energy-intensive indoor space. The *Phantom House*, like the *Slow House*, in the end remained unbuilt; the clients separated during the course of the design process.

At around the same time, Julie Taubman shared with Dennis Freedman her frustrations about the first attempts to build the East Hampton house; she expressed similar feelings to another friend, Richmond Burton, an architect turned artist who lived in East Hampton and whose work the Taubmans collected. Burton turned out to have studied architecture at Rice University along with Charles Renfro, and he, like Freedman, suggested that Julie and Bobby speak with Diller Scofidio + Renfro. With a recommendation now in hand from two different friends, the Taubmans went ahead and arranged a meeting with Liz Diller, Ricardo Scofidio, and Charles Renfro in the spring of 2010 at the DS+R studio in the Starrett-Lehigh Building on the far west side of Manhattan.

"We met with them here in the studio and showed them the unbuilt *Slow House* and our small residential oeuvre of mostly unbuilt houses," Renfro said. "I think we got them excited about the work of the studio. And we were excited by Julie's effervescence." Although all three partners were involved at the outset of the project and through design development, Renfro would end up taking the lead through technical development and construction. He seemed to connect easily with Julie Taubman in a way that Phifer had not. Renfro was particularly taken with Julie Taubman's passions for both high and low design.

Diller + Scofidio, *Phantom House*, Proposal for a single-family house in Phoenix, Arizona, composed of twin dwellings, a linear, indoor house that hovers above a protected outdoor house with parallel domestic functions, 2007

He found her intriguing, not to say bold. "She had nerve, being willing to pull the plug at the last minute [on the Phifer project]," he said. "Of course, that was both good and bad. What if we were the next to go?"

These concerns were put aside just a few weeks after that initial meeting. In July 2010, the Taubmans and DS+R agreed to start to work together on the project, but this time the Taubmans committed only to a limited contract that called for the architects to produce a set of conceptual ideas. The understanding was that if one of the ideas seemed worth pursuing, they would negotiate a new contract for more extended design work. And if nothing seemed right, they would part with no hard feelings.

Renfro and Diller went to East Hampton to look at the Two Mile Hollow Road site, which they found exciting and beautiful but, Renfro would later say, "awkward—it was narrow, with lots of height restrictions and major setbacks." The portion of the beachfront property on which the notoriously demanding Village of Easthampton would permit actual construction was just a slim rectangle amounting to less than 20 percent of the total acreage. And it was largely perpendicular to the ocean, which was why Thomas Phifer had set the long, rectangular volumes of his design with their short ends facing the dunes.

"The restrictions were the opposite of what you'd want—we had to figure out how to overcome the narrowness," Renfro said. The challenge was made somewhat easier, Renfro thought, when the Taubmans said during their initial meeting that they were willing to forego a garage and a tennis court. "They didn't want the trappings of a major villa," Renfro said. "They wanted modernism on the beach, a house without all the bells and whistles that had overtaken the Hamptons." What excited Julie Taubman, Renfro remembers thinking, was the spirit of a house like the Double Diamond House in nearby Westhampton Beach, designed by Andrew Geller in 1959, an exuberant geometric form made of wood and glass, both playful and daring, which in recent years has come to be thought of as emblematic of a certain period of postwar Hamptons modernism when anything seemed possible and overt expressions of wealth were frowned upon.

How, Renfro wondered, could the spirit of that house, the notion that freshness mattered more than grandeur, be interpreted in terms appropriate to the 21st century? What did modern even mean in the 21st century? The Double Diamond House looked like two boxes turned and balanced on their edges. The Taubmans, Renfro knew, were certainly not going to build anything quite as basic as the Geller house, nor anything that looked remotely like it. And in any case DS+R's long-standing interest in technology would hardly allow the firm to build a simple box of wood, glass, and concrete blocks, which seemed primitive by contemporary standards. Nostalgia for mid-century modern was not what motivated the Taubmans. But the essence of the Double Diamond House was not its shape, famous as it had become; it was the way in which Geller used the house's presence on the dunes to justify a radical play on formal geometries that broke away from most of the conventions of housebuilding. This pair of boxes balanced on edge looked, at first glance, like a house that should not be able to stand up. Like a person doing acrobatics on the beach, it interpreted being on the dunes as license to break from normal decorum. A shape that you would never produce for a house in an urban context here exemplified a casual, open life on the beach, and a willingness to break away from convention. That was the lesson to take from the Double Diamond, Renfro felt, not its actual appearance. The challenge would be to find the 21st-century equivalent of the Double Diamond.

Liz Diller remembers it somewhat differently. "The houses Julie was attracted to were organic, and the houses she dismissed were geometric," Diller recounted. "While single-surface buildings and complex geometries were the rage at the time, and design was liberated by new digital platforms, we were looking for more rigor. The unbuilt *Slow House* was a frustrating reminder of the house that got away. The Taubman house was a way to return to plastic form." Renfro recalled that "Julie was definitely most interested in the organic houses such as Kellogg's High Desert House in Joshua Tree, but we did spend a lot of time speaking about the Geller House and other Long Island modern houses as well. Part of our interest in rethinking the organic forms of the mid-century era stemmed from changes in design and fabrication technologies in the digital age."

It was the beach in East Hampton, the shape of the dune itself, that would provide the inspiration, DS+R decided. "We wanted the natural geometry of the beach to dictate form," Renfro said. "In that sense, it was different from the formal geometry of Geller," or the other early postwar modernists who built boxes or triangular or round shapes. The flowing lines of the dunes were inherently sculptural and dynamic—they were organic, and Julie responded to that. They also invoked the architecture DS+R knew Julie Taubman valued most, buildings like Eero Saarinen's TWA terminal at JFK Airport, and his Dulles Airport outside of Washington, D.C., as well as houses by Couëlle, Lautner, and Kellogg. They felt that echoing the rolling shapes of the dunes would ensure that the house looked nothing like the boxy modernist houses of the previous century.

By the end of August, Renfro and his colleagues Quang Truong and Michael Etzel, along with Liz Diller and Ric Scofidio, had produced four different but related schemes, essentially four variations on curving, fluid forms that they felt would express the spirit of the East Hampton dunes in built form. They called the first one, arguably the most experimental, the 'Mobius' scheme, since it was an attempt to create what Renfro called "one continuous space that by its form would create privacy. It was a courtyard house with curved-up ends," almost like a rocking horse. The second version, known as the 'Roof' scheme, was a set of pavilions under a large overhanging roof, whose form somewhat echoed the undulating dunes. Then there was what the architects called the 'Dunes'' scheme, which also reflected undulating,

Diller Scofidio + Renfro, Blue Dream, early concept studies for different schemes: Mobius, a single continuous space with rooms made through sectional adjustment; Roof, a mega-roof with individual dwelling pavilions beneath; Dunes, dwelling spaces formed by alternating undulations; Ravioli, a large organic dune-shaped roof filled with private dwelling spaces over an undulating landscape with shared dwelling spaces

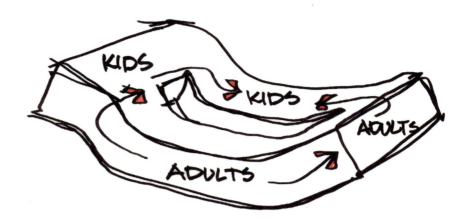

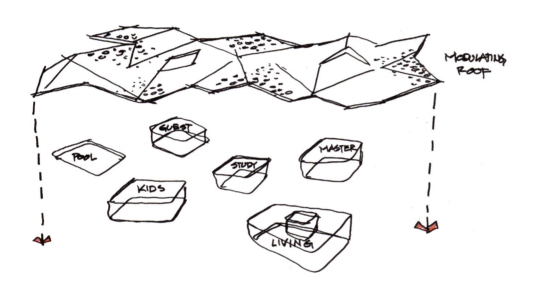

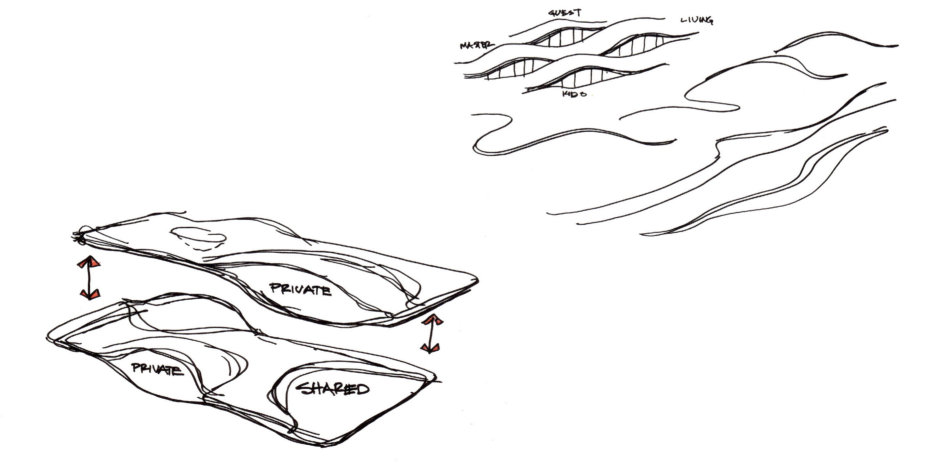

Starting over

rolling dunes, this time in the form of four distinct, mound-like structures, effectively separate pavilions without the single, unifying roof. And finally, there was the version they called the 'Ravioli' scheme, in which a few private spaces were tucked above and below a large, central, rolling space that would wrap around them like pasta envelops a bite of ground meat or cheese. It could be described both as more concise and concentrated than the other schemes, and more complex.

The Taubmans preferred it, largely because it allowed the interior to feel like a continuous, flowing space and still provided for certain spaces to be set apart. By September, DS+R was fully into the schematic phase of the design, turning the Ravioli scheme from a concept into an architectural design, which meant trying to resolve the conflicts between their conceptual idea, the limitations of structural materials, and the Taubmans' needs for various kinds of living space.

"Julie said this should be a beach house, nothing formal, but she said she wanted to enclose the kitchen, because their chef often cursed, and Bobby's study, because he was prone to occasionally talking loudly on the phone," Charles Renfro said. The master suite was tucked into a fold upstairs, while the children's bedrooms were set below the main level, and a guest suite tucked into a space underneath the master suite. Everything was enveloped within a larger, undulating structure, the form of which flowed continuously from ceiling to walls to floor. There were very few vertical walls in the house, and indeed, few straight lines of any kind. There were also no conventional divisions between the walls, floors, and ceilings. In DS+R's models and drawings, while the floors were flat, they curved upwards into walls, and then curved again into ceilings, all running together as if poured into a vast mold.

The Ravioli scheme also allowed DS+R to emphasize views of the dunes and the Atlantic Ocean—at one point Renfro called the house "a machine for viewing"—and to create an innovative structure that would allow the building to stand largely free of columns. Developing that structure would prove to be complicated and far more difficult than anything else about the house. But it was essential, not only to ensure that the ocean views from the house

Diller Scofidio + Renfro, Early sectional sketch of the Ravioli concept

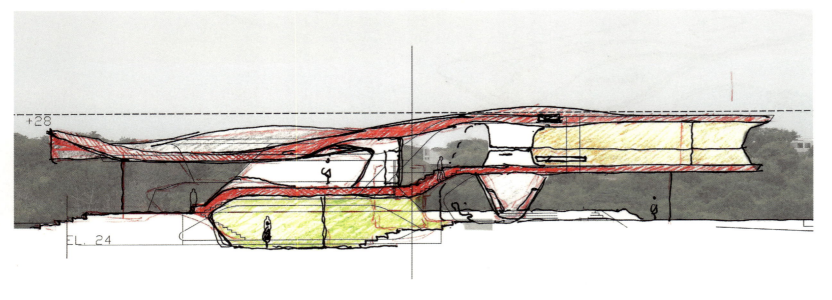

would be unobstructed, but also to realize Julie Taubman's preference for a sculptural shape that did not resemble the boxy geometric forms of earlier modern houses. And since so much of Diller Scofidio + Renfro's work had always been experimental in nature, making a design that would require meeting a new technological challenge did not appear unreasonable. It seemed, in fact, like the only way in which both the client and the architect could get what they wanted.

"We were trying to make a new image for the ocean, to have some of the gestural feeling of Saarinen's TWA terminal, but also to have a casualness," Renfro said. "It doesn't look like anything else except maybe TWA." If the overall form of the house owes a slight visual debt to TWA, it also evokes the work of Kellogg, as well as some of the work of Lautner, the disciple of Frank Lloyd Wright whose sculpted houses of the 1960s, mainly in southern California, represented a similar attempt to push the boundaries of modernism toward more fluid, organic form. Many of Lautner's projects, like DS+R's design for the Taubman house, have enormous roofs that stretch over living spaces and curve down to the ground. The architects were drawn to the work of Lautner—some of whose houses turn up in Julie Taubman's various files of architectural inspirations—as they developed the design for the Taubman house. At the same time, they were aware of the work of Jacques Couëlle, the eccentric architect of vacation houses in the south of France, whom Julie Taubman had brought to their attention. The Taubman house would be more rigorous than Couëlle's picturesque organicism, and far more a product of technology, but it would nevertheless retain at least a distant connection. Renfro also notes that the team had been thinking about one of Le Corbusier's final projects, the Heidi Weber Pavilion in

The house responds to the primary views of the beach and dunescape, with every room looking out to a particular and unique view

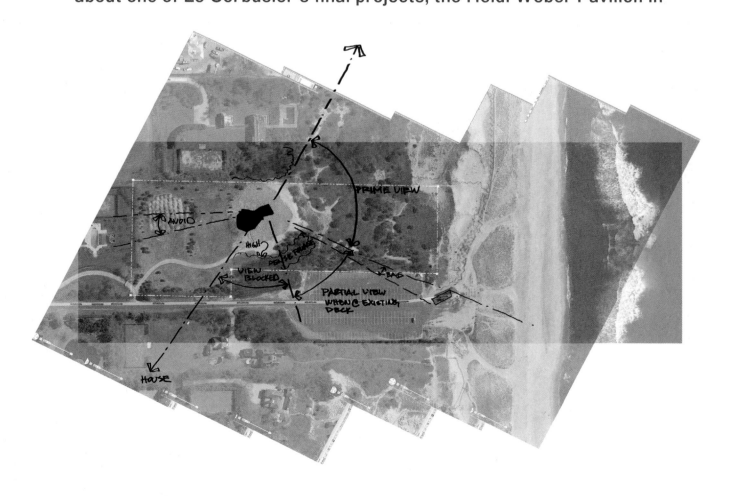

Starting over

Zurich, a museum completed in 1967, in which small structures containing galleries are grouped under an enormous roof supported by columns, which is, for all intents and purposes, an independent structure. "We were thinking of it as an inspiration for big roof projects in which the roof has its own integrity," Renfro said.

The Weber pavilion, now called the Centre Le Corbusier, is geometric, with boxy forms and angles that, if anything, evoke the mid-century modern houses of eastern Long Island more than the swooping, curving forms of TWA or the houses of John Lautner and Jacques Couëlle. The final design for the Taubman house would look far more like Saarinen and Lautner than Le Corbusier, with a combination of geometric precision and sensuous curves that Renfro would come to call "mathematical organicism," a phrase that Bobby Taubman particularly liked. In two words, Renfro had summed up DS+R's attempt to connect the rational and the emotional, to make the house precise and technologically driven, and at the same time sensuous and natural.

Later, Renfro would describe what he felt DS+R was doing as "taking modernism into organicism," a journey that might be thought to evoke a very different late Le Corbusier building than the geometric Weber pavilion, the architect's chapel of curving concrete at Ronchamp, in eastern France, in which he tried to evoke a spiritual aura through what he called "ineffable space." In whatever way the organic aspect of the Taubman house is

Concept models reflecting different approaches to the Ravioli scheme

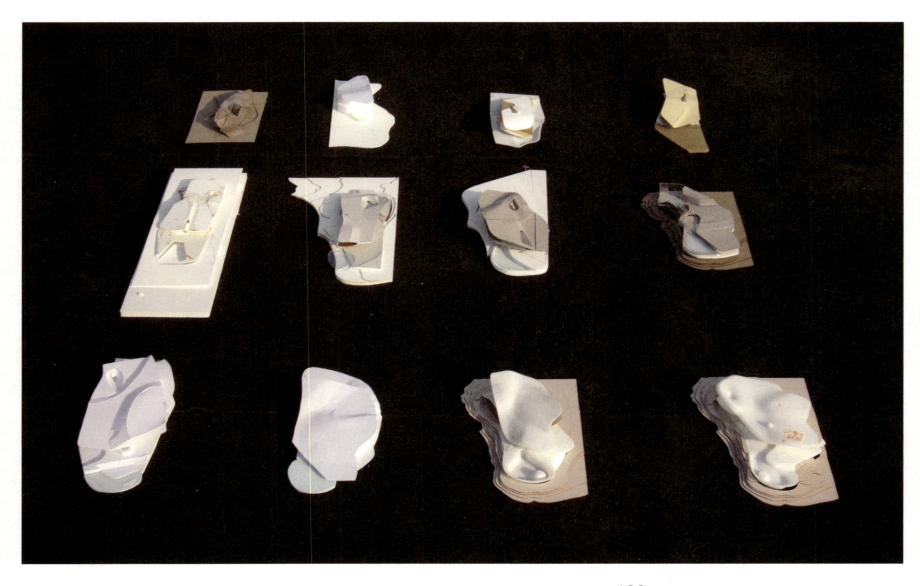

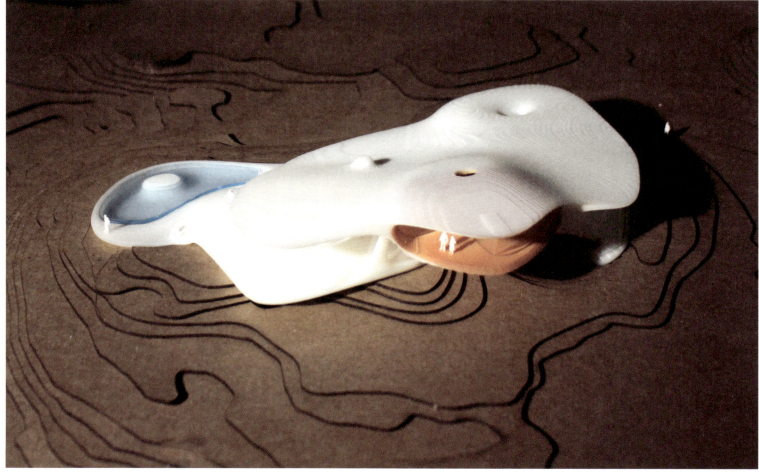

ABOVE
Schematic design model of the ground floor showing the continuity of the exterior dunes landscape to the interior

BELOW
Schematic design model with the roof in place, showing the private spaces embedded in thickened pockets

described, it also bears a resemblance, at least conceptually, to a far more radical design than even TWA, or any of the built works of Lautner or Kellogg or Le Corbusier: Frederick Kiesler's *Endless House*, the visionary but never-realized, visionary project that Kiesler developed on and off from 1947 until his death in 1965. It was Kiesler who set out to blur the distinction between floors, walls, and ceilings, as DS+R would do. Kiesler went so far as to eliminate conventional rooms altogether, and make his entire structure seem almost like an inhabitable version of a human organ. The models for the biomorphic *Endless House*, many of which are in the collection of the Museum of Modern Art, suggest something that did not so much look constructed as grown naturally.

The Taubman house, of course, was real and not imaginary; it would have to house a real family, and it would have to be built, and to stand for decades in a challenging climate at the water's edge. It would be full of practical challenges that Kiesler, designing to demonstrate an idea rather than to fulfill a real architectural program, could ignore. And the Taubman house would have to connect closely to the landscape and almost appear to emerge from it, unlike the *Endless House*, which Kiesler envisioned as hovering slightly above the ground, like Mies van der Rohe's Farnsworth House. (The connection between Kiesler's *Endless House* and Diller Scofidio + Renfro would be underscored in 2015, when the Museum of Modern Art, which holds portions of Kiesler's archive, mounted an exhibition entitled *The Endless House*, which brought together conceptual work that reflected Kiesler's spirit, including DS+R's *Slow House* of 1981.) Still, even though the Taubman house would hug the earth and appear to flow out of the dunes rather than float above them, it was hard not to look at the early models DS+R put together without thinking that at least part of the architects' goal was to evoke the feeling of the *Endless House*. Kiesler's goal was to create a building that would look not as if it had been put together piece by piece, but rather as if it had just flowed onto its site as one enormous, continuous form. And DS+R wanted to achieve the same thing.

Holly Deichmann examining the completed study model for the schematic design phase

DESIGNING A STRUCTURAL EXPERIMENT

ABOVE
Design development model showing bedrooms sandwiched in the roof and nestled in the dunes

BELOW
Structural study for a steel 'egg-crate' roof solution

Frederick Kiesler, Jacques Couëlle, and Eero Saarinen were not the only influences shaping the design DS+R was producing for the Taubmans. By the second decade of the 21st century, digital technology had become an established force in architecture, and it was far easier to engineer and build unusual shapes made up of complex curves than it had ever been before. Computers could not only enable the construction of unorthodox shapes, but had also become sophisticated enough to guide the process of design. Swooping, oozing forms became common enough so that one architect who was an early practitioner of the genre, Greg Lynn, named it 'blob architecture', a term that stuck, though it came to be used dismissively as much as admiringly. Lynn would have an indirect influence on the house: he was Quang Truong's professor at Yale, where he instilled in Truong a deep interest in computer-driven design and new composite materials. Truong developed an expertise in both which would make him a critical part of the team as the design of the house was developed, and then later, as the team addressed the question of how to build it.

The making of unusual shapes was hardly a new architectural frontier: what Frank Lloyd Wright called "breaking out of the box" had been a goal of many architects for much of the 20th century. But for a long time, technology made it difficult to engineer and construct such shapes, particularly those with few straight lines, and the combination of imaginative architects and determined clients that allowed projects like Saarinen's two pathbreaking airport structures to be realized was rare. By the 21st century, digital technology had changed the paradigm, and complex curves were no longer exotic; if anything, they threatened to become too common. The Dutch architects Ben van Berkel and Caroline Bos had already designed a house of complex, intertwined spaces they called the Möbius House (1993–98), prefiguring the name DS+R gave to one of the schemes for the Taubman house.

The architects faced several problems as they began the process of converting their concept for the Taubman house into a finished design. First, they had to satisfy the Taubmans' programmatic needs, which included multiple children's bedrooms, guest quarters, and a large master suite, as well as the garage, gymnasium, and tennis pavilion they originally indicated they were willing to omit. While the program was becoming ever more elaborate, Julie Taubman remained firm in her view that she did not want the house to be either as large or as formal as the structures that were going up all around it in East Hampton. She reiterated her commitment to making it new, not making it grandiose.

Renfro and his partners wanted a radical design for the house at least as much as Julie Taubman did. For them, this would be more than a matter of appearance: creating what might become the first work of blob architecture in the Hamptons was not how they wanted the house to make its mark, and neither would it be consistent with the rest of DS+R's oeuvre, which tried to go beyond striking visual images in order to use architecture as a means of exploring social and cultural ideas. A one-of-a-kind sculptural shape might be beautiful, and its sinuous, sensual lines would surely distinguish the house from the geometric shapes of earlier Hamptons modernism, but for DS+R, this would not be enough to define the house as something they would consider truly new. There had been relatively little genuinely avant-garde architecture built in the Hamptons for years, and they did not want shape alone to be the calling card of their design. For it to be like no other house, they felt, it would also have to be built in a way that no house had been built before.

For DS+R, it was essential that the roof structure, rolling over the entire house, be column-free to allow the space beneath to flow unencumbered. The roof, floors, and walls would merge, not unlike the way they did in Kiesler's *Endless House*. But here, DS+R had the added challenge of trying to fit the many demands of a real and complex building program into unobstructed flowing space, which would seem inherently inconsistent with the nature of fluid space. How could the various separate spaces the Taubmans required—an office/study, private rooms for guests and children, and a kitchen relatively out of sight and out of hearing—be compatible with a huge, wavy roof that was free of interior supporting columns and conventional inside walls? "We wanted to make a structural experiment—unobstructed views and no visible vertical support," Renfro said. "There needed to be a 'look ma, no hands' quality."

The key to the organization of the house was in the original concept for the Ravioli scheme, which called for the roof to be not the 'topping' of the structure, but more like a kind of wrapping, a solid mass that would curve and fold around the various spaces. The blurring of traditionally distinct elements begins on the exterior, where the outside walls and the roof are one continuous flowing surface, at times curving down to meet the ground to become solid wall and provide support, at other times leaping up to leave large openings that are filled with glass, and at still other times almost appearing to rise out of the ground. It could probably best be described as a kind of shell.

On the south side, facing the ocean, the house appears to be two stories high; at the front door, on the north, it reads as a single story. Inside, multiple levels are tucked behind that single-story entry, but there are no conventional staircases. Instead, portions of the structure rise from below, with steps carved into their masses, like staircases carved out of stone mountains. A mound on the right leads up to the study, which is tucked like a balcony over the main living space, while a larger mound on the left leads to the master suite, and another set of stairs slips down to children's bedrooms on a lower level, which are partially below the grade at the front.

Neither a conventional floor plan nor a conventional section drawing is of much help in understanding how the interior of the house works, although it could be described as split-level, since the entry is at an intermediate level, and all the main living spaces are either up or down a half or a full flight of stairs from there, not unlike the mid-century suburban tract houses that this house in no other way remotely resembles. There is a certain pleasing irony in noting a connection between Diller Scofidio + Renfro, the Taubmans, and suburban development, since DS+R have long been interested in the relationship of popular culture to high culture, and suburban shopping centers are the basis of the Taubman family business. The house is not, however, a comment on suburban architecture, even obliquely, and in the end, its layout is best understood by thinking of the interior as a continuous flowing sequence of spaces, tucked in and around and behind and under and above one another, set in or on mound-like forms beneath the undulating shell of the roof, almost all of them positioned to take advantage of the ocean and landscape views that are visible in the broad expanses of glass that fill the voids between the sections of structure.

The bedrooms and bathrooms have doors, and the study is enclosed in glass to afford acoustical privacy, but everything else is open. The kitchen, which is set beside the dining area, is largely set apart in response to Julie Taubman's wish not to hear the noises that accompany cooking, though it is not fully enclosed. It is relatively compact, but then again, the entire house as constructed comprises roughly 8,500 square feet of living space and under 10,000 gross square feet (not including the separate garage and gymnasium)—small by current standards for oceanfront houses in the Hamptons, if hardly the modest modern pavilion that Julie Taubman often said she had hoped to build.

Once DS+R figured out how to shape and mold the spaces to allow distinct private areas to co-exist with open space under the large, flowing roof, there remained the question of how that roof was to be constructed. If the highly complex spatial arrangement of the final design was largely based on the original Ravioli scheme (and while it went through years of refinement, the fundamental ideas remained consistent), there was no such model to follow when it came to the actual structure. "Liz, Ric, and Charles imagined the ideas for their buildings first, and figured out how to build them later," said Quang Truong, who spent a decade working at the firm. "Diller Scofidio + Renfro were artists, true artists, but they hadn't built a house of this complexity, and their drawings were conceptual. They were not enough to build from," Ed Bulgin said after he saw the initial designs, which made clear how the building should look, but offered only some preliminary notions as to how to construct this enormously complex, continuous shell structure that would curve up and around and enclose and define all the spaces while being supported only at certain points where it met the ground on the outside. It was clear that it would be necessary to work with structural engineers to try to find a construction technique that was affordable and made use of the expertise of the local contractors and subcontractors.

The ultimate solution would be up to Ed Bulgin. While the Taubmans felt obliged to interview at least one other local builder before they committed to hiring Bulgin again, they leaned strongly toward continuing to work with him, and not only because of his long-standing interest in taking on unusual construction challenges, which would be even more useful if they went ahead and built DS+R's design. They also felt that Bulgin had been exceptionally gracious when the Taubmans cancelled the initial plan to build Thomas Phifer's design. Notwithstanding all the preparations he had made for the start of construction, all they had received from Bulgin in 2008 was a relatively modest bill for his time. He said he hoped that the Taubmans would build a house someday and would turn to him again; in the meantime, he had plenty of other work.

At the beginning of 2011, the architects sent preliminary plans to Bulgin and to one other local contractor, Wright & Company, for a rough estimate of pricing. They would continue to work with both Bulgin and Wright for a year, as plans were refined; both the Taubmans and the architects felt more comfortable having competing estimates to work with, and two different contractors to respond with comments and suggestions about the plans. In the end, they both seemed capable, but of course only one contractor could be hired to build the house, and in May 2012, with the start of construction just a few months away, the Taubmans, always respectful of Bulgin since the aborted Phifer project, followed their instincts to stay with him and signed a construction contract. Now, Ed Bulgin would be more than an estimator and a negotiator: he would have to figure out how to get the house built.

When Bulgin first saw DS+R's plans, the design looked, he said, like "a sculpture you attempt to live in." He was prepared, he said, to try and build the house, but there were so many uncertainties that he was unwilling to offer a traditional fixed price contract. "The drawings weren't developed enough to lock it all in," he said. "I said we could do some things at a fixed price, and for others we would have to wait, and some others couldn't be guaranteed at all"—like the roof. Bobby Taubman said he loved the way the shape of the house looked in the model DS+R produced of the final design, but that he wasn't sure, even with all his knowledge of construction, how the swooping roof and exterior shell could be built. "They said it would be done in concrete, with a single pour," he recalled. "I said there aren't enough cement trucks in all of Long Island to allow this much of a continuous pour."

The architects liked the notion of concrete, not only because it has historically been used for many buildings with challenging shapes like Saarinen's TWA terminal, but also because some form of sand or gravel is a basic ingredient of its makeup, and thus the house could feel connected in an even deeper way to the dune on which it was set. "The idea was that the shape could literally be cast out of the dunes, that you could use the sand to create the forms," Truong said. It was an oddly romantic notion for as intellectually rigorous a firm as Diller Scofidio + Renfro, though imagining the roof as literally being formed from the dunes was, if nothing else, an appealing piece of symbolism. The Taubmans allowed DS+R to do some preliminary work with Ed Bulgin and Dan Sesil of LERA, the eminent structural engineering firm that was already engaged on the project, to try to figure out

ABOVE
Structural study for an all-concrete roof concept, LERA Consulting Structural Engineers

BELOW
Sketch of structural concrete section, Dan Sesil, LERA Consulting Structural Engineers

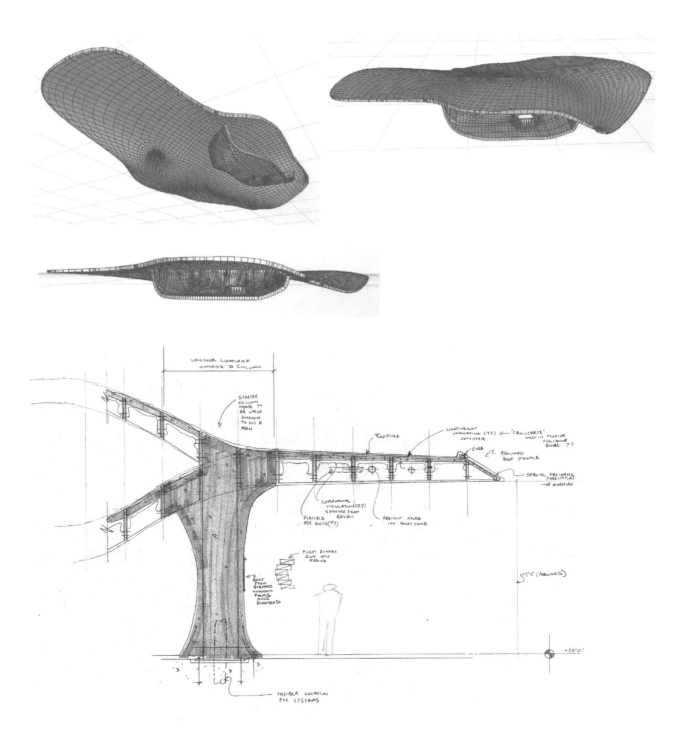

a workable system. Concrete had been a favored building material for John Lautner, Kendrick Bangs Kellogg, and Jacques Couëlle, as well as Oscar Niemeyer, the Brazilian architect who both Taubmans also admired. Using concrete seemed to make all the more sense if their work, like Saarinen's TWA, was to be considered among the architectural antecedents of the Taubman house.

But using poured concrete in this instance was proving problematic, given the potential weight of the enormous expanse of concrete that the plans called for. A roof made entirely of poured concrete in the shape DS+R had designed would have been too heavy to allow the free and open space that the architects envisioned. It would have required supporting columns, which would have changed the feeling of the interior significantly. The space frame would be hidden within the curving roof structure, but vertical columns would intrude on the central open space of the house. "The goal was to make the architecture disappear at the end of the living room—you would have an unobstructed view to the water, and you wouldn't feel like the architecture was there," Charles Renfro said. And this was much more than a personal concern of Renfro's. Keeping the view to the ocean wide open and not allowing it to be interrupted by metal mullions in the windows or supporting columns had always been a high priority for Bobby Taubman, who was determined to find a solution that would allow an unobstructed vista of the Atlantic.

Alternate study for a 'bundled steel tube' roof concept proposed by Dan Sesil, LERA Consulting Structural Engineers

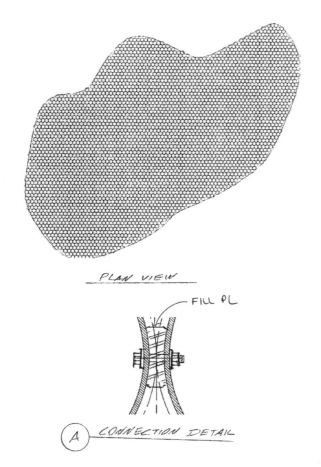

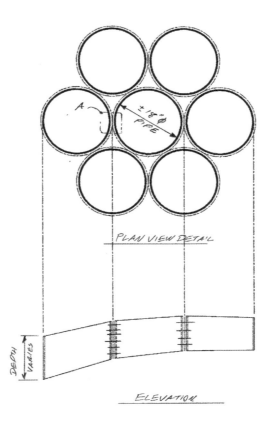

A further issue was that using the sand from the site as the basis for the concrete formula was not yielding the right kind of conrete, and there were additional problems in sequencing the different portions of the roof and external structure. It would have needed to be cast from top to bottom, meaning the heavy top pieces would require support while the bottom pieces, which reached down to the ground to anchor the sturcture, were cast below them. At the point, poured concrete was no longer an option. Bulgin briefly considered making the structure out of gunite, the sprayed-on concrete often used for swimming pools, which he thought could be an effective way to achieve the shape DS+R had designed. But futher studies showed that gunite would not have lessened the weight enough to avoid the need for supporting columns, and the idea was quickly discarded.

By then, Bulgin had already begun to dig the foundation, and DS+R, for their part, were not ready to give up on their design. In their view, it was one thing to be flexible about the number of bedrooms or the size of the kitchen, but quite another to consider changing the basic aesthetic concept of the house. They wanted it to look a certain way, and the Taubmans had approved their design. As the team struggled with ways in which to meet the challenges of concrete without making any significant changes to the appearance of the house, David Currie, who was Ed Bulgin's job superintendent, had a question: couldn't the roof be molded out of the kind of new, lightweight carbon fiber material that is used to make super yachts and jet fuselages, Currie asked. Currie had a lot of experience with boats, and he knew that yacht construction was far ahead of architecture in the development of new

The goal of the roof structure was to provide unobstructed views of the ocean beyond the dunes

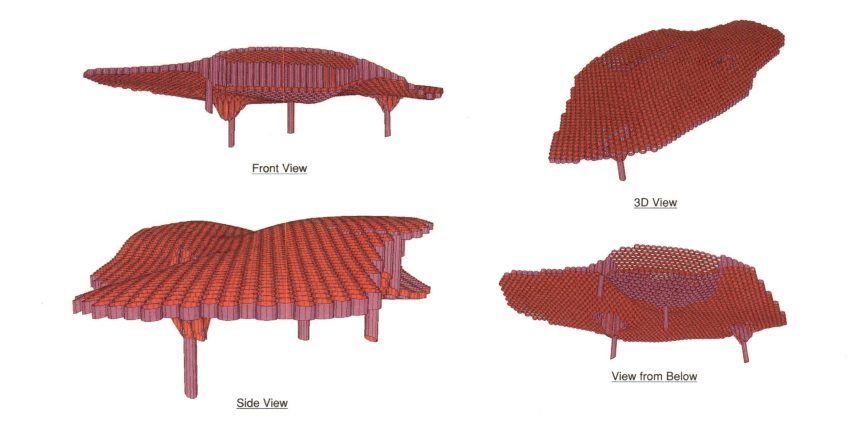

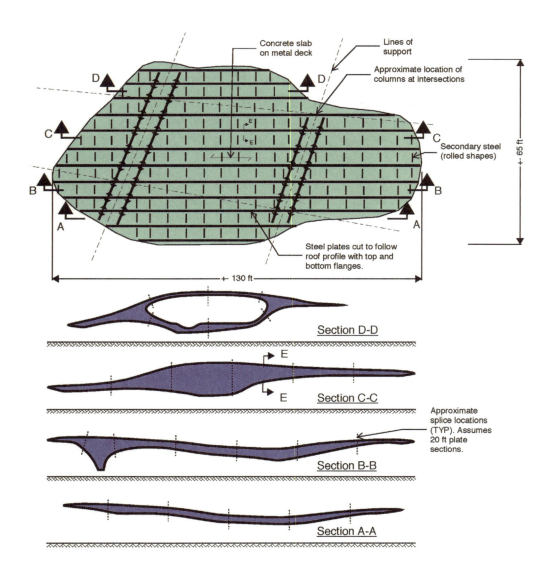

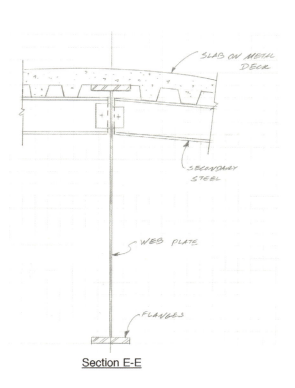

ABOVE
Digital model of the bundled steel tube proposal

BELOW
An alternate proposal for a hybrid concrete and steel roof system with tapered girder profiles

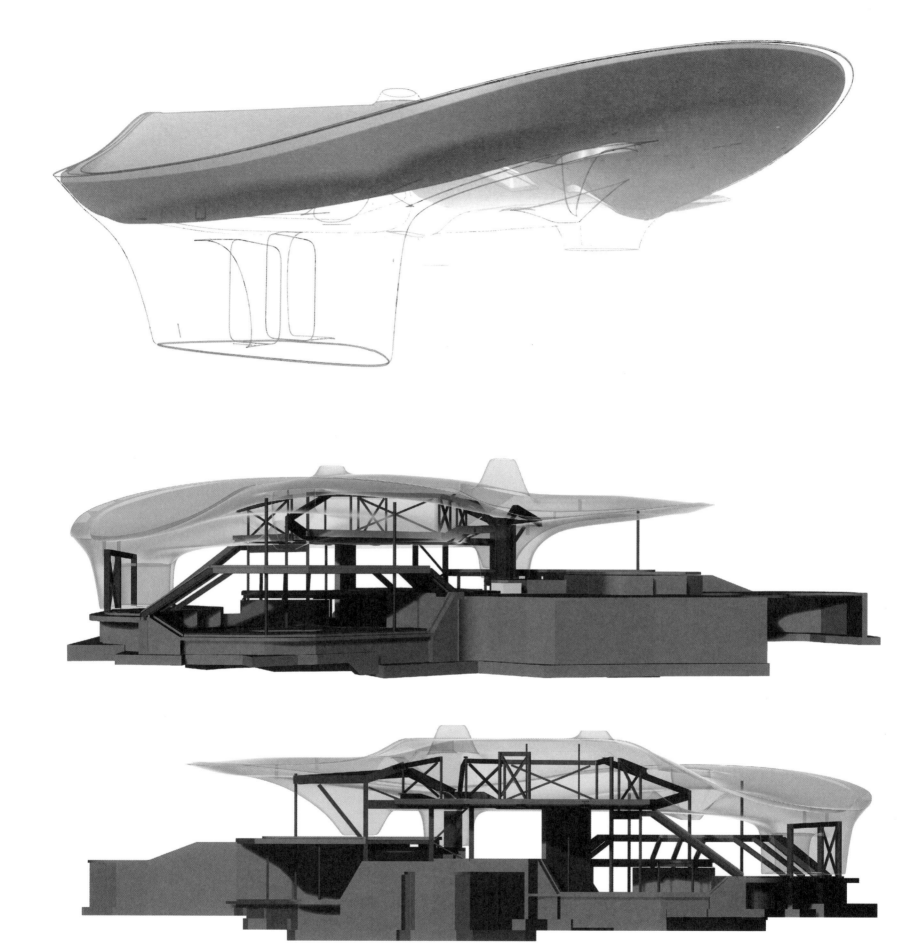

ABOVE
Model of the foam interior of the monocoque structural system devised for the house

BELOW
The lightweight compound roof allowed for a minimum of steel supporting elements

Designing a structural experiment

composite materials that were light in weight and as strong, if not stronger, than conventional construction materials. These advanced composite materials were what Quang Truong had studied with Greg Lynn, and Truong had maintained his interest in their development as he began his career as an architect. He and David Currie became the prime advocates for replacing concrete with a new high-tech material. It was an idea that would ultimately turn out to be the best option, and it would change the entire trajectory of the project. The move to a lightweight composite material broke the deadlock over concrete and cleared the way to build the superstructure.

DS+R, far from being upset at the notion that the design for the concrete roof they originally envisioned had to be jettisoned, were delighted. The original sketches for the house had contained a notation suggesting fiberglass, which the architects did not pursue at first, thinking concrete would be more practical. But DS+R was more than willing to try any new material Currie and Truong were advocating. They saw the change as a way of making the house an even more radical piece of design, lighter by far than the original scheme. "We ended up with what was the most innovative roof of anything we considered," Renfro said. "When we ran into the problems, we did not revert to a conventional solution—it actually pushed us farther." Nothing would have to change in the shape that DS+R had conceived and the Taubmans had agreed to build. What would change would only be what that shape was made of—a material developed for boats and jet planes which here, would be used more extensively in the making of a work of architecture than ever before.

A MATERIAL BREAKTHROUGH

Diller Scofidio + Renfro were architects, not engineers, and when they departed from their core job of giving form to a series of programmatic requirements—which in the case of the Taubman house meant a set of spaces for family leisure beside the ocean—it was usually to engage in some degree of social critique. They liked to challenge the underlying premises of architecture, and they were uncomfortable with the notion of the architect as a professional who unquestioningly accepts the ambitions of politicians, corporate executives, and real estate developers, and sees his or her role as simply expressing these ambitions in physical form. It was no accident that they worked most often for institutional clients such as museums or cultural organizations, the kinds of clients for which a certain degree of social criticism was often an expected part of their mission. DS+R liked making memorable, highly expressive shapes, but they never wanted their architecture to be considered driven by the crafting of shape alone, and it was not. Since the founding of their practice, they have tried to make their buildings expressions of how architectural form can reflect new ways of interpreting traditional architectural programs. They never wanted their architecture to be thought of as pure sculpture.

Architectural clients have always been somewhat self-selecting: a conservative corporation would be no more likely to want DS+R to design its headquarters than the firm would want to take on such an assignment. In its early years as a studio doing largely conceptual projects, they had few clients of any kind, let alone people of great means. But in recent years, the firm's renown has attracted clients like David Geffen and Eli Broad, both billionaire Los Angeles art collectors and philanthropists who would

Diller Scofidio + Renfro, The Broad, Los Angeles, 2015

probably never have considered DS+R as architects for the businesses through which they made their fortunes. For Eli Broad, however, who hired the firm shortly after the Taubmans did, a DS+R building would send just the right message for the new public museum he was building to house his art collection in downtown Los Angeles, which he hoped would rethink the traditional form of the art museum. At The Broad, DS+R, with Liz Diller as partner-in-charge, reconceived the museum by making the storage areas of the immense Broad collection the centerpiece of the building and devised a way of moving through the building which ensured that every visitor passed by the storage galleries and saw them in juxtaposition with the exhibition spaces. The escalator gliding up through the mass of the Broad building would bear a certain resemblance to the staircase that had already been designed to lead to the master bedroom of the Taubman house, underscoring the extent to which the house would serve as a kind of design laboratory for DS+R.

The Broad was intended to suggest a rethinking of the art museum, but no such equivalent act of rethinking was possible, or even desirable with the Taubman house. For all of Julie and Bobby Taubman's love of architecture, it was still a family house, with the customary program of a house, and there was only so much reconceptualizing that could be done about that. DS+R couldn't make the family closets the centerpiece, or the kitchen, or the swimming pool. The Taubmans had no desire to eliminate any of the components that make up a conventional house, even as they emphasized how little they wanted any element of their house to look conventional. That was a further design challenge for the DS+R team: they had to make a house

Diagram of the cinematic exit through the Broad's archive

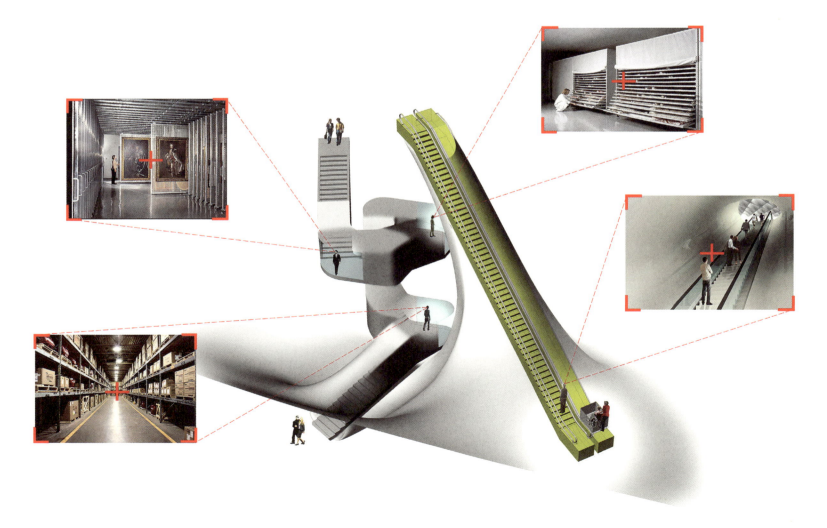

that looked different, even though it was to be made up of the same functional components as any other house and had to operate in much the same way. The house could not indulge in the social critiques of many of DS+R's other projects. There was no way to deny that it was an expansive villa on the ocean, created for well-to-do clients who, for all their advanced taste, wanted to be surrounded by comfort, not conflict. The oceanfront site was, of course, spectacular, but paradoxically, that restricted the design further, since the Taubmans expected the house to respond to the presence of the ocean in the obvious way, which is to say they wanted much of the internal organization to be based around the view. The public spaces like the living and dining areas would have to be on the main level with the bedrooms located elsewhere, as in a traditional house.

To the extent that the house would be a critique of existing houses, then, it would not be by rethinking the program of a traditional house, but by offering a different physical form, a new kind of shape and appearance. But how, then, to avoid making it seem like an arbitrary shape, a piece of sculpture, the very thing that DS+R did not want to create? It became increasingly clear as the design process moved forward that the house would establish its radical identity in large part by how it would be constructed, and through the architects' openness to new types of building materials and technology. Charles Renfro was not being disingenuous when he described the decision to give up on the original concrete roof as helping the project; the inability to make the roof work as it was first designed opened the door to making the house more truly the radical piece of design that Julie Taubman had hoped for.

But it also meant that more of the project would fall into the hands of engineers and technical experts. Renfro was not an expert in the new technologies that were now going to be used, and while Truong had more knowledge of them, he was an architect, not a structural engineer or a fabricator or a software engineer, all of whom would turn out to be essential to the process. Dan Sesil, the structural engineer at LERA assigned to the project, had a long history of helping architects, including DS+R, figure out how to get unusual structures built, but he knew that the proposition of building the exterior of this house out of a new composite material would require additional highly specialized expertise. The right material would have to be chosen from among the thousands of high-tech composite materials manufactured, and then the roof and exterior would need to be redesigned in order to be constructed of the chosen material, all the while ensuring that it would look almost identical to the original concept.

Determining how a roof that had been conceived to be made of concrete should be constructed out of a new substance that had rarely been used as a building material would, not surprisingly, delay the project for several months and add considerable cost. It would ultimately involve crossing the Atlantic Ocean to find David Kendall, a British engineer whose company, Optima Projects, Ltd., specializes in working on advanced structural

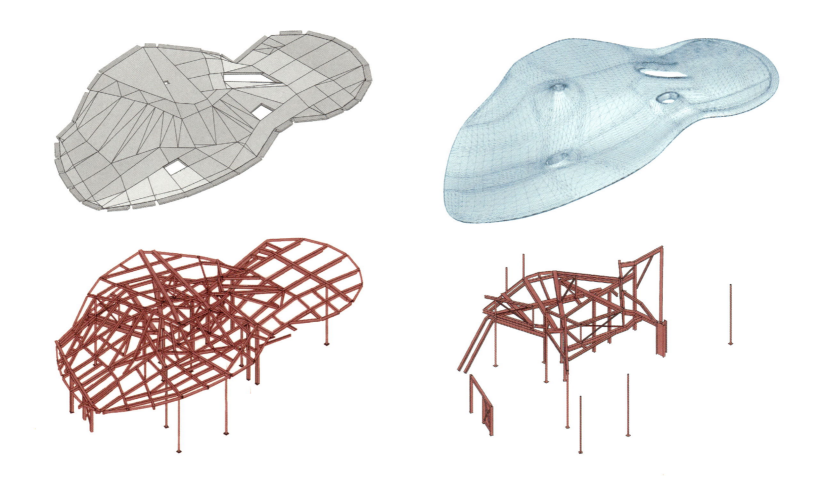

ABOVE
Diller Scofidio + Renfro and LERA, Comparison of the steel/concrete system (left) and the foam monocoque structure (right) reveals a tremendous reduction of steel

BELOW
Mock-up of the monocoque roof constructed of foam from recycled water bottles clad with fiberglass skin, Calverton, Long Island, New York

A material breakthrough

designs with new forms of composite materials; and then, it would be a matter of going almost as far from New York in the other direction to find Janicki Industries, a company located 70 miles north of Seattle which specializes in composite materials and is known for its work in the aerospace industry, fabricating missiles and jet planes, as well as making hulls for advanced racing yachts. Janicki has done much of its work for the United States Department of Defense, and even manufactured portions of spacecraft that flew to Mars. In the end, the roof structure would be overseen by a far-flung team that consisted of LERA, based in New York; Optima Projects, Ltd., in Lymington, England; Janicki in Sedro-Woolley, Washington; Truong and Renfro at DS+R in New York; and David Currie and Ed Bulgin at their office in Southampton, a few miles west of the project site in East Hampton.

The team settled on a material called Glass Fiber Reinforced Polymers (GFRP), effectively fiberglass, as the most appropriate for the house, and devised a complex system, more than two feet thick, of layers of glass fiber placed over milled blocks of polyethylene terephthalate foam. Ed Bulgin likened the combination of fiberglass and foam to an enormous surfboard. The glass fiber and the vinyl ester resin used to coat it were chosen, Quang Truong would write later, "for their structural capacity and their ability to meet specific performance criteria set out in the building codes," while the foam offered not only resistance to wind shear, but "a sustainability bonus of being completely composed of recycled plastic water bottles."

Though it was massive, it was relatively light, and the decision to use it allowed the engineers to use only a fraction of the steel that had originally been envisioned to provide structural support. Between the reduction in steel and the difference in weight between the concrete and the GFRP composite material, the overall weight of the house dropped by 220 tons, an amount that Ed Bulgin estimated was roughly two-thirds what it would have originally weighed.

The complex calculations that would determine the precise form of the curving structure and ensure that it would meet the project's structural requirements were made in CATIA, an advanced software platform initially created for the aerospace industry. CATIA had been pioneered in architecture by Frank Gehry, who first used it to assist in shaping and fabricating the pieces of titanium making up the facade of his Guggenheim Museum in Bilbao, Spain (1997). But Gehry was using the software to allow him to engineer metal, a familiar building material, into an unusual shape. Its use in the Taubman project was to figure out how to use a very different material, not a customary building material, but one that would unite architecture with CATIA's aerospace origins. As the design team played with variations on the shape of the continuous, connected roof and exterior wall structure, the software could quickly calculate the impact of even the most minute change in the structural integrity of the building. If Renfro wanted to see the effect of making the curves on one side a bit softer, for example, or the windows a bit larger, the CATIA software could determine the effect these changes would have on the structure's weight, its ability to handle wind and snow, and the extent to which changes in temperature would cause it to expand and contract. On the oceanfront, there was the challenge of temperatures that could vary by as much as 30 degress during a single day. And the entire structure had to be designed to survive the risk of a Catagory 5 hurricane with 185 mph winds—not an easy requirment for a conventional building system, let alone an experimental one. The pressures of the harsh, potentially storm-tossed oceanfront climate mattered more than they might in a more conventional building, because the house would have no sheathing on top of its structure to provide an added layer of protection, the way wood siding or shingles do. As Quang Truong would write, "the finished skin serves as the structure, and vice versa."

All the calculations made with CATIA had a single goal, which was to find a point where the architect's aesthetic preferences and the efficiency and strength of the structure met—to have the simplest, lightest structure possible consistent with the appearance of the building that the architects had envisioned. The team experimented constantly with small design variations, each of which was run through the CATIA system to create a model that would test the impact of any kind of design change on the overall structure and to ensure that it could handle the necessary wind loads, thermal loads, and so forth.

In one case, information revealed through the CATIA software analysis resulted in the decision to insert a narrow metal column discreetly into the southwest corner of the living room, facing the ocean, despite the architects' preference for having no interior columns. This area contained the broadest expanse of glass in the house, and the CATIA calculations revealed that the roof would require further support at the point where it spanned the wide expanse of glass unless it were reinforced with carbon fiber, changing the glass fiber formula that had already been selected as the structural material, or the weight of the roof were further reduced by some other means. Another option was to lighten the roof by cutting back a cantilevered section on the other side of the living room, where the roof extended beyond the house toward the pool area. A third option would have been to break up the wide expanse of glass by inserting supporting pieces, or mullions, between the sections of glass, but Renfro and the Taubmans had agreed from the beginning that they wanted the glass to appear continuous, and they did not want to interrupt the view with even thin vertical elements. They all felt that the aesthetic of an uninterrupted view was critical. The option of a shorter cantilever on the pool side did not please anyone, since it removed both a visually important element and a useful source of shade to the west. And changing the composite mix would have added significant cost and the potential for further delay to an already expensive project. In the end, the Taubmans agreed that a thin, freestanding column, set just inside the corner of the glass, would be the best option.

As it turns out, the column is barely visible and has no real impact on the view. Indeed, as an aesthetic decision it could be justified as a unique accent at a unique point in the house, the southwest corner of the main living space—more of a gentle punctuation mark than an unwelcome intrusion. A similar column was placed, equally discreetly, at the east end of the house in the lower-level guest suite, and another supporting column was tucked into the structure of the three-part fireplace that opens to a seating alcove, the main dining area, and the outdoor dining area. How the thin living room column beside the glass wall came to be, however, reveals the complexity of the decision-making process for the project. The designers had to propose each option for changing the structure, discuss it with the engineering team, run calculations in the CATIA software to determine its impact, and then present it to the final decision-makers, the architectural partners in charge, and of course, the Taubmans, who had the final say. "Each cycle of decisions took a long time, because every time we considered a change, we had to run it past Julie Taubman and Bobby Taubman, Charles Renfro, Liz Diller, and Ric Scofidio," Quang Truong said. "And we did this a dozen different times."

The process was occasionally complicated further by the involvement of Alfred Taubman, who was close to both his son and his daughter-in-law, and who prided himself on his ability to think about architecture in both practical and aspirational terms. This house was not anything like any of the buildings he himself had built, but Alfred Taubman, who had been trained as an architect, admired the ambitions behind it, and both Bobby and Julie Taubman turned to him often for advice. Decades earlier, he had engaged in a legal battle

The finished superstructure of the house, with roof spans of up to 30 feet on 11 points of support

with Richard Meier when the house Meier designed for him in Palm Beach had problems of water infiltration that Alfred Taubman believed were the result of a design error, and he thought of himself as alert to things that architects might overlook. He reviewed the plans for the East Hampton house at almost every stage and made frequent suggestions. When DS+R added a roof deck atop the master bedroom, it was Alfred Taubman who worried that the stairs might allow water to make its way down from the roof and encouraged the architects to develop a watertight hatch entry instead, like something that would be used on a ship. At other points, he made suggestions that affected the design of the master closet and the wine cellar.

The complexities of a design and construction process that involved multiple family members as well as numerous outside consultants could be frustrating, and were especially so to the engineers at Janicki, who were accustomed to corporate clients like Boeing, or government clients like the Department of Defense, or clients with the singular focus of racing yacht owners. In each of these cases, a clear hierarchy set the direction of a project early, and there were firm technical parameters for decision-making and little margin for change. Such precision is rarely the case in the organization of most architectural projects, particularly residential ones, where the personal needs and wishes of clients change frequently, are not always based on quantifiable metrics, and in the case of married couples sometimes reveal that the clients themselves do not fully agree. Personal taste is not a factor in the fabrication of a jet fuselage, but it looms large in the design of any house.

Julie and Bobby Taubman met frequently with Renfro and his colleagues to refine the design. The complex design process was smoothed considerably by the arrival at DS+R of Holly Deichmann, who joined the firm a few months after the Taubmans became clients. As project director for the house on Two Mile Hollow Road, she coordinated internal design matters at DS+R as well as communications between the Taubmans and DS+R and within the rapidly growing team of professionals involved with the realization of the house. Before joining DS+R, Deichmann had worked with Peter Gluck, in the Gluck+ office in Manhattan, where she oversaw the design and construction of a six-building family compound in the Adirondacks which, if not as ambitious a work of design as the Taubman house was shaping up to be, posed at least as many challenges. Deichmann combined a commitment to the cutting-edge work of DS+R with an ability to work with the firm's aesthetic and a level of management skill not typically possessed by architects of a sophisticated design bent. Early on, Deichmann began keeping detailed notes on every design meeting in Detroit or New York, and in one case, she met with Alfred B. Taubman in his Michael Graves-designed office on Fifth Avenue to discuss the project.

The firm's notes show that while the basic concept of the Ravioli scheme carried through from the initial presentation to the final design, there were numerous discussions, debates, and changes. Some were minor and almost comic, such as a long-running question of whether the house should have a pizza oven, which Bobby Taubman wanted to include, but Julie Taubman did not. The pizza oven started out as an element connected to the three-part fireplace, which opened onto the dining area, the living room, and the outdoor dining terrace, but when that proved too complicated and there was no room for it in the kitchen, Julie told the architects to eliminate it. Then it reappeared outside next to a barbecue grill in response to Bobby Taubman's insistence that it somehow be included. Indoor planters also came and went several times during the design process, but they were never included in the final design, despite Julie's preference for bringing plants indoors, largely because DS+R could never come up with a design that they felt was original enough. "Everything felt too much like Frank Lloyd Wright," Holly Deichmann said.

Other issues, including an extended discourse about materials for the interior, went more to the heart of what the house would be. At a meeting in March 2011, Liz Diller suggested that the floor and the mounds that rose from the floor to enclose lower-level rooms should be made of a material like concrete, so that they would appear monolithic, and that built-in furniture be made of wood or another warm material. Bobby Taubman questioned the concrete floor, worried that it would give the house a cold feeling. He was willing to live in an unusual house, but not in what could feel like an industrial building. Julie expressed concern about the use of too many materials, and said she preferred a single material that would cover both the floor and the wall mounds, and for a period the architects investigated the use of mesquite wood, which they felt could have been applied successfully on the sloping form of the mounds and the interior stairs cut into them. "But Julie didn't want wood. She had a vision for the house that was all one material, and light colors," Deichmann said. Discussions about the best material for the interior would not be resolved for another two years, but

LEFT
Preliminary proposal of carved end-grain wood in the master bedroom

RIGHT
Mock-up of sculpted end-grain mesquite wood

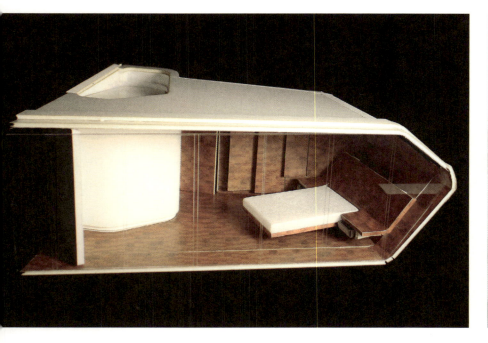

eventually any thought of wood was abandoned in favor of a highly specialized, very unusual and durable type of plaster made by the French company Marius Aurenti, which had the flowing, sculptural qualities of concrete, but with greater warmth. It had to be applied by hand, and once in place, would tie together the floors, the stairs, and the mound shapes as seamlessly as the composite material used on the outside of the house. David Currie discovered it while on a vacation in the Caribbean. The material visually resembles the fiberglass composite of the structure itself, so that on the inside of the house, the ceiling, walls, and floors feel continuous both with each other and with the exterior. Michael Lewis and Ed Bulgin visited the Aurenti factory in France to discuss fabricating a variant of its plaster for the house, and the company sent workers to East Hampton to show Bulgin's team how it should be applied.

In April 2011, the Taubmans invited the architects to meet at their house in Bloomfield Hills, Detroit, so that they could see the furniture and art they had collected. The conversations about materials for the interior continued, and another subject came up, which was just how much glass the living room should have. Bobby Taubman wanted as much glass as possible, to maximize the view of the ocean. Julie Taubman preferred a larger, more enveloping roof, and said that she wanted the house to feel sheltering. The views would be better if they were framed, she said, offering an implicit argument for somewhat less glass. In the end, both Taubmans got most of what they wanted: the entire south wall facing the ocean is of glass, but the roof structure is large and enveloping, both open to an expansive view and framing it at the same time.

Interior materials selection for the house

Every aspect of the long process of creating the roof and external structure was in one sense a venture of unusual, if not to say extraordinary, ambition in advanced design and technology. The point, however, is that the drive toward technological innovation had to coexist, sometimes awkwardly, with issues common to even the most mundane residential design projects: what does the family want, what are its priorities, and how do the clients choose to balance their aesthetic preferences with functional needs and budget? It was a reminder that the remarkable level of ambition that the Taubman house represented brought no freedom from the most common and everyday issues that have always been a part of residential design.

Although the roof was designed to appear as a continuous, unbroken form, echoing the shape of the dunes and then flowing down to the ground, it was constructed out of panels that were seamed together as the house was constructed. It could not have been otherwise, since the panels were manufactured in Washington state, and had to be limited to a size that could fit on a flatbed truck so that they could be shipped across the country to East Hampton. The panels were not standardized: the flowing shape, the fact that some of the panels were on the roof and others on the facade, as well

ABOVE
Fabrication and placement of the monocoque roof, formed of 27 segments of CNC-milled foam blocks joined together with a fiberglass surface

BELOW
Foam roof block at the fabricator

140

ABOVE
Concrete foundations, May 2013

BELOW
Steel support structure, May 2014

Construction sequence: December 11, 2012 to August 10, 2016

A material breakthrough

Arrival of a roof segment
on the construction site

ABOVE AND MIDDLE
Placement of a foam block roof segment

BELOW
Roof structure completion, view from the beach

145

as the need to interrupt some of the roof sections for vents, skylights, and chimneys, and for some of the wall sections to accommodate joints with glass, meant that every one of the 28 panels was unique in both shape and thickness, making the challenge of fabrication all the greater.

Assembling them would be no easier than designing and fabricating them. When the panels began arriving in East Hampton, each making the journey of 3,022 miles, almost as far as any trip within the continental United States could be, on its own flatbed truck, Ed Bulgin erected a structure of plastic over the foundation, effectively a temporary building within which |the actual building would be erected. There, Bulgin's site supervisor, Mike Cunningham, could line up the structural panels in the order in which they would be assembled, devise temporary supports for the various pieces during installation, and proceed free of interruptions from the weather. The actual installation of the panels onto a steel framework was so complex that it required the assistance of crews from Janicki who were experienced with boatbuilding, as well as advanced geospatial locating systems to guide the precise positioning of each panel. The need for absolute precision made it, Bulgin said, "a delicate process—there was no tolerance."

But it worked as planned. Not only did all the pieces fit together as designed, they also all remained intact, and Bulgin would later note that after several east coast winters, no cracks had appeared in the structure, which continued to look as if it had been made as a single, molded object. That, of course, had been the goal, and its achievement was a clear sign that the decision to make the building out of a composite material instead of concrete had been the right one. As Truong would later write in his book about composite materials in architecture, paying homage to both the design and the postwar heritage of East Hampton, Diller Scofidio + Renfro had succeeded at giving the Taubmans "a conceptually audacious building located in this historic testing ground for adventurous modern houses."

OPPOSITE
Construction view from the living room

ABOVE
Roof assembly in process

Roof assembly in process

Building wrapped for winter construction

ABOVE AND BELOW
Roof touchdown points made of Glass Fiber Reinforced Gypsum (GFRG) in the living room (above) and in the roof form and stairs (below)

A material breakthrough

Stairs between the main living space and the master bedroom

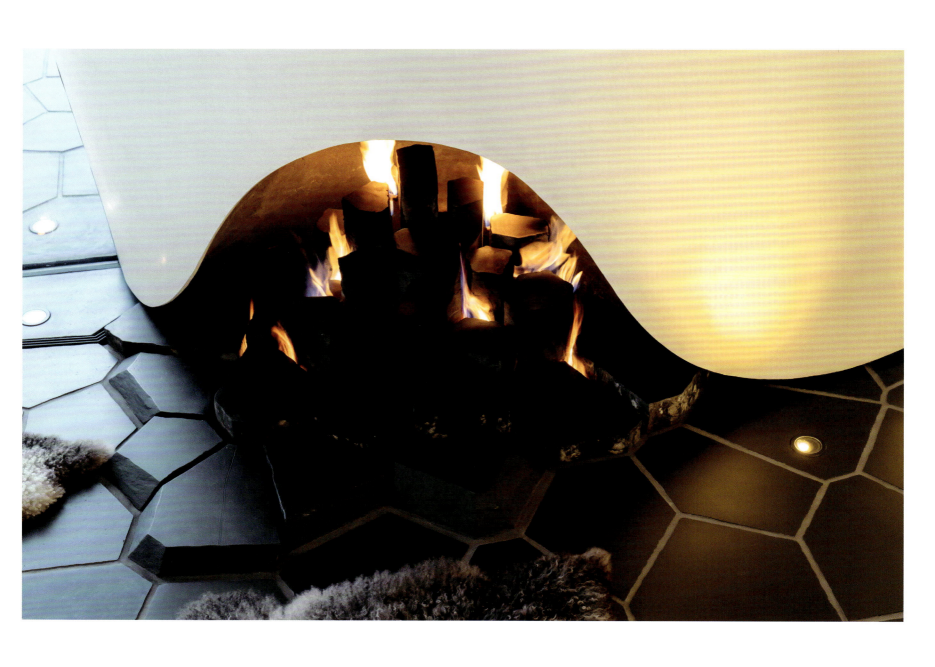

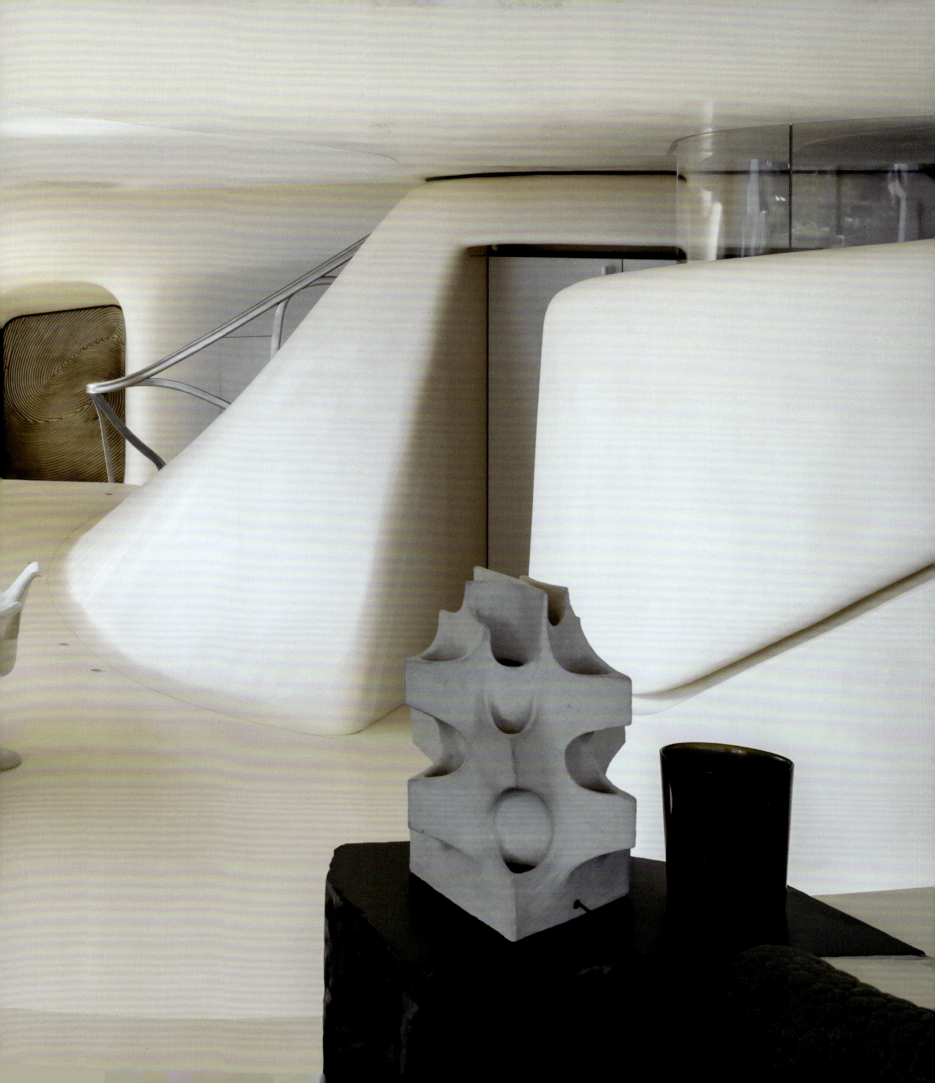

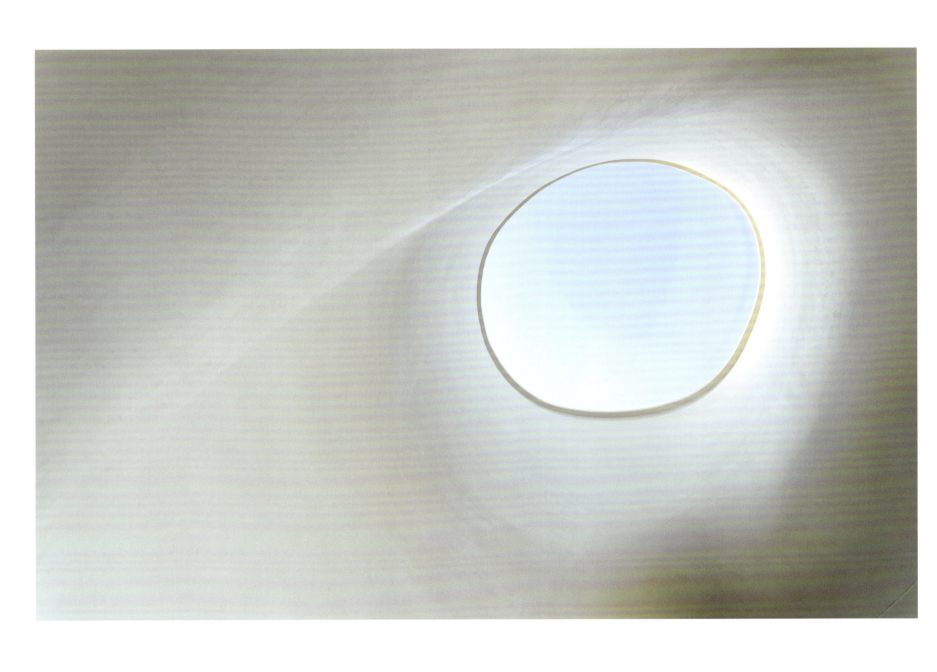

GESAMT-KUNSTWERK ON THE ATLANTIC DOUBLE DUNES

The intensity that surrounded the exterior of the house, with its international team of engineers, consultants, and fabricators, had an equivalent on the inside. Long before work began on the fiberglass panels of the exterior, Julie Taubman had begun to think about what the interior of the house should look like, and here, as with the structure, the goal was to find experts from around the world who could work comfortably with Diller Scofidio + Renfro and shared their vision for the house. It was no more a job for a conventional interior designer than the house itself was a job for a conventional architect, and while the Taubmans did not expect DS+R to furnish the rooms by themselves any more than they expected them to engineer the structure by themselves, they knew that the wrong partner could undermine the impact of the architecture. They needed to find an interior designer who admired DS+R and understood their architectural intentions, and just as important, understood Julie Taubman's design sensibility. It was not in her nature to want furnishings to disappear or defer entirely to their surroundings; her own collecting had always been bold, and she envisioned the house as a showcase for many of the objects that she had collected over the years, and others that she would commission. It was clear that there would not be much, if any, art—the large expanses of glass and absence of straight, flat walls meant that there would be almost no space available to display paintings, and in any case, as Renfro put it, "Julie wanted the house to be the work of art." It would be the house itself, and the furnishings within it.

There were a couple of false starts with designers who did not, in the end, meet Julie Taubman's criteria. Then, in conversation with Linda Dresner—the Detroit-based fashion retailer whose single-minded commitment to cutting-edge fashion and design had made her both a friend and a role model to Julie and whose minimalist shops in Michigan and New York were revered in the architecture and design world—Julie learned about a designer who was assisting Dresner with the interiors of the minimalist concrete house she was building with the architect Steven Sivak in Birmingham, Michigan, near the Taubmans' home in Bloomfield Hills. His name was Michael Lewis, he lived primarily in Paris, and he had built a significant international practice as an interior designer working for wealthy private clients around the world whose projects were architecturally distinctive and required a knowing and sympathetic eye. Lewis had no 'signature' style; he prided himself on respecting the direction set by architects and then providing furnishings that would enhance rather than compete with the underlying architectural intentions. Unlike most designers who cater to an elite base of clients, he seemed to eschew publicity: he had no website, his work had not been published in a book, and he was not a figure of the gossip columns. He positioned himself more like a treasured resource that the cognoscenti could pass around to each other.

Julie first asked her friend Dennis Freedman, who was on a business trip to Australia, if he could detour through Paris en route back to New York to meet Lewis and see what he thought of the designer, and whether Lewis would be a suitable match for both Julie herself and DS+R. The two men met in Paris, and Freedman was impressed with Lewis's knowledge and sensitivity about architecture and design. He suggested that Julie meet with him as soon as she could get herself to Paris. Not long afterward, she met Lewis for tea at the Hotel Costes. She liked him, and decided that there should be one more step. She asked Charles Renfro to fly to Paris to have his own meeting with Lewis, just to ensure that they were compatible. Renfro, too, was struck by Lewis's knowledge, but also by his boldness. "He found artists who seemed modest and were making amazing things," Renfro said. Lewis was able to convince Renfro that he had no desire to fill the house with objects that would undermine the architect's intentions (the fear of every architect when an interior designer is brought in), and in March of 2014 Lewis joined the design team. He traveled to New York to meet with DS+R and to study the plans for the house.

At that point, the interior layout had been decided but not completely finalized, and many key decisions, such as the material that would be used on the floors, remained to be made. Lighting in particular was an open question; the plans called for downlights to be recessed into the curving ceiling, but Julie Taubman did not like rooms lit from above, and Michael Lewis agreed, which meant that multiple lamps would have to be added to the interior designer's scope of work. Julie did not object at all: lighting was an area in which many of the designers she collected excelled, and there was plenty of opportunity to light the rooms with different kinds of modern lamps, both vintage and new. In the end, there would be only one ceiling-mounted lighting fixture anywhere in the house, a 350-pound abstract chandelier of white bronze suspended over the dining table (pp. 166–67), which Julie commissioned from the sculptor Darcy Miro. Miro would later describe the piece as "a meteor, a barnacle, a homing beacon, ambiguous and contemporary in color, as perforated and sculpted as the moon."

Darcy Miro's Dunes Fixture during the final stage of the casting process, overseen by lead finishing specialist Peter Ross, Polich Tallix Fine Art Foundry, Rock Tavern, New York, August 2015

The room arrangements had gone through multiple iterations, as they do in almost every custom-designed house, even though the general split-level layout of the interior, with the main living space on the south side facing the ocean, a half-level above the entry on the north side, remained consistent throughout the design process. At various points, rooms expanded and contracted, caught between the Taubmans' desire for a wide-ranging program and Julie's preference for a house that, however striking as a work of design, would still appear modest in size by comparison to the ever-larger mansions that were its neighbors on the East Hampton dunes.

Both the living room and the kitchen were small by comparison with the equivalent spaces in most of the nearby houses. The bedrooms for the Taubmans' four children—Alexander, Ghislaine (known as 'Gogo'), and twins Sebastian and Theodore—were tightly configured into the lower level of the house. There was to be only one guest accommodation, in the guest suite below the master bedroom. For additional guests, the Taubmans decided that they would use a small wood-frame house in the center of East Hampton village that they had purchased as temporary quarters during construction. Julie had the exterior charred, using the traditional Japanese method of *yakisugi*, a technique of burning wood slightly to give it a black overlay. The striking charred wood, along with deep red painted trim, gave the house distinction among its weathered shingle neighbors as Julie prepared to use it for overflow guests and additional storage space once the house on the dunes was finished.

Julie decided to call the new house 'Blue Dream'. The name was, in part, a tribute to her friend Elmore Leonard, who died in 2013, as construction was beginning. Leonard was fond of the strain of marijuana known as 'Blue Dream', which is said to enhance creativity. At his death, Leonard was working on a novel he had titled 'Blue Dreams', and Julie, who liked to give every house she owned a name, recalled how much Leonard had enjoyed visiting the Taubmans' Thunderbird House in Rancho Mirage. She proposed naming the East Hampton house 'Blue Dream', a name that paid homage to Leonard and at the same time had just the right amount of sauciness, not to say irreverence, for her. Bobby Taubman agreed, and from that point on, the house became Blue Dream.

Lorraine Wild with Benjamin Woodlock, Blue Dream logo, 2016

She would display a similar mix of affection, respect, and wit when the Taubmans took over Alfred Taubman's Alden Dow house in Bloomfield Hills, Michigan, which they renovated after his death in 2015. She had a close relationship with her father-in-law, whom she called 'Big Daddy', and she decided that her family's new house should bear the initials 'BDH', for Big Daddy's House. If that was something of an inside joke, a name used mainly by the owners, Blue Dream would be different. Before the house was complete, the Taubmans commissioned designer Lorraine Wild to produce a Blue Dream logo, written in a relaxed script, that would be embroidered in pale blue on towels and napkins used throughout the house, printed on notepads, and engraved into the wooden gate at the entrance to the property.

Julie's determination and her worldliness, not to mention her intensity, were a good match for her father-in-law, whose large ambitions had fueled his career in real estate development, his art collecting, and his purchase of Sotheby's. Each saw the other as a kindred spirit, a larger-than-life iconoclast whose best trait was an openness to new ideas. Julie certainly shared Alfred Taubman's fondness for acquisitions: she purchased modern furniture, lamps, rugs, and objects at such a rate that she had to lease warehouse space near her home in Michigan to accommodate her inventory. Like William Randolph Hearst, who filled a warehouse in the Bronx with artifacts he acquired in Europe which he would only later figure out how to incorporate into one of his residences in New York or California, Julie bought what excited her in the hope that she would eventually find a place for each piece, and in the meantime was content to have them stored in Michigan.

What distinguished Julie Taubman from William Randolph Hearst, however, was that her purchases, however striking and unusual, were not huge lots of mixed quality as Hearst was known for, but careful and deliberate purchases of rare items that reflected her highly personal connoisseurship. Her warehouse became a kind of accidental museum of 20th-century design, reflecting Julie's preference for the daring and surprising rather than the conventional lineage of Bauhaus and Danish Modern. And for Michael Lewis, it became the most valued place from which to source objects for the East Hampton house. "What was so brilliant about her was the quantity and variety of what she had purchased," Lewis said. "She had stock"—in other words, an enormous inventory of objects that she had bought over the years simply because she liked them. "She was always buying, wherever she was. She knew that she would find interesting stuff, both high and low....
I remember once saying we needed something for one of the kids' bedrooms," Lewis said. An Ettore Sottsass lamp from Memphis, the postmodern design movement from the 1980s, was the sort of offbeat thing Lewis had in mind. "And it turned out to be in her inventory. It was there."

One of Julie's most striking purchases was an extraordinary assemblage of yellow sofas by the Chinese artist Yin Xiuzhen, which she bought when she accompanied Bobby Taubman on a business trip to Beijing. The piece, called *Life Raft*, consists of a set of chairs upholstered in found textiles, ganged together in a metal frame that includes tailpipes, intended to evoke the experience of immigrants huddled together (pp. 160–61). Like much of Yin's work, the piece uses old textiles and objects that evoke her childhood in Beijing, in this case with an agenda that is more political than nostalgic. When Blue Dream was finished, Lewis and Julie placed the Yin piece at the far end of the living room, making *Life Raft* quite literally a seating area overlooking the ocean. As an object, its frame loosely evokes a group of Le Corbusier's classic 1928 *Grand Confort* chairs pushed too closely together and then covered in inexpensive fabric instead of expensive leather: a modernist cluster in which something seems slightly amiss. That is exactly the kind of thing that inevitably caught Julie Taubman's eye—many of the most notable objects in the house, like the *Lady Grey Chair* by Lucy Dodd in the guest room that consists of pigment on cotton thread placed over a chair frame by Marcel Breuer (pp. 210–11), or the *Blue Rope Meltdown Chair* by Tom Price in Theo's bedroom (p. 215), look like classic modernist pieces that have decomposed, or been altered in some way.

So, too, with one of the most ambitious of the many pieces that the Taubmans commissioned for the house, the dining chairs by Chris Schanck which were made using vintage Eero Saarinen Tulip chairs. Julie and Michael Lewis asked Schanck, an alumnus of the 3D Design program at the Cranbrook Academy of Art, if he would consider modifying Saarinen's famous chair, which she loved but felt had become, like many popular modern pieces of furniture, so familiar it was almost a cliché. Schanck's sensibility, which his gallery described as "finding a comfortable place between the distinctions of dilapidation and assemblage, individual and collective, industrial and handcraft, romanticism and cynicism," very much echoed Julie's own.

LEFT
Furniture designer Chris Schanck and collaborators modifying vintage 1950s Tulip chairs by Eero Saarinen in Schanck's studio on Buffalo Street, Detroit, 2016

RIGHT
Saarinen-Schanck dining chairs, 2016

Bobby Taubman wanted swivel chairs "and we couldn't find anything better than the Saarinen Tulip," Michael Lewis said. Not only was the Saarinen chair the best swivel dining chair available, the design's central rounded base avoided the problem of a forest of legs that might compete with the form of the dining table. Schanck was skeptical about altering original Saarinen chairs, Taubman recalled, but he agreed to work on two of them as a trial. The Taubmans ultimately purchased 44 vintage Tulip chairs on eBay, and sent a pair to Schanck, who proceeded to cut holes in their curving plastic forms, then re-coat them with a new carbon fiber material, giving them a flocked surface. The experiment was judged a success, so the artist continued with the rest of the group, cutting a different pattern of holes in each chair so that every one of the chairs could be considered a unique, handcrafted object, both a Schanck and a Saarinen. The Taubmans had managed at once to pay homage to Saarinen, Julie's favorite 20th-century architect, and commission a new work of art that, like the house itself, used both the oldest and the newest materials available. The Saarinen-Schanck chairs exemplified Julie's sensibility: they celebrated the classic modernist heritage and undermined it at the same time, breaking it apart as a way of pushing it forward.

The chairs were placed around one of the most important commissions Michael Lewis initiated, a twelve-foot-long curving outdoor dining table by Joseph Walsh, a furniture artist based in County Cork, Ireland, who mainly works in wood and stone. His work is soft and lyrical; it does not have the edginess of pieces by many of the artists and craftspeople whose designs the Taubmans have collected, but it is hardly traditional. What is most remarkable about Walsh's furniture is how he coaxes out of graceful, curving lines a startling sense of newness, as if wood or stone had never been carved in such a way before. For all their sensuousness and elegance, his pieces seem as radical as anything else in the house. "I had been working with Joseph for many years, and I saw that what Charles Renfro was

LEFT
The large block of marble extracted from the Joyce Family Quarry at Connemara, County Galway, Ireland, used to make the Eximon outdoor dining table designed by Joseph Walsh, January 2015

RIGHT
Joseph Walsh's Eximon outdoor dining table during the carving process at the quarry, January 2015

doing with the house was so similar to what Joseph was doing with furniture," Lewis said. "I thought how great it would be to put them together. He was working in the same way as Diller Scofidio + Renfro, on a smaller scale."

Indeed, Walsh, like DS+R, often imagines sinuous shapes before he is entirely sure how they can be made. He works with engineers as well as woodworkers and stonecutters to determine a process for crafting each piece, and he takes pride in the experimental nature of his work. This has arguably made him the central figure of a contemporary craft movement in Ireland. "What are we making in the 21st century, and why?" is the question Walsh likes to believe underlies his work.

He would come to have as great an impact on the interiors of Blue Dream as any other designer, creating a wide range of furniture as well as architectural details like the hand-crafted wooden door handles that took the place of conventional metal hardware in some rooms. His curvaceous sculptural lines ended up determining not only the amoeba-shaped Exilumen dining table, but also the Eximon outdoor dining table, its main section carved in Connemara marble and permanently anchored to the ground. Walsh designed lighter extensions made of aluminum and cast resin, which could be attached to the main marble table to make one long, voluptuous composition, placed separately as stand-alone tables, or removed for storage. The nearly 20-foot-long block of Connemara marble Walsh used was the largest ever extracted from the Joyce Family Quarry in Connemara, County Galway, Ireland. In another nod to technology that was critical to Blue Dream, the engineering firm of ARUP oversaw the extraction, devising a means of injecting the huge slab of marble with resin so that it would not break as it was cut out of the quarry.

For the master bedroom, Walsh designed the Erosion bed crafted of olive ash and with a white oil finish that subtly evokes driftwood; a pair of travertine Erosion end tables, a cabinet crafted out of resin to hold the television in the master bedroom; a long, curving handle of wood for the glass door of the study, and another for the glass door of the wine cellar. Each piece was unique. Walsh, who is largely self-taught, does not design pieces except on commission, and Michael Lewis and the Taubmans encouraged him to expand his scope of work for the house to include certain things he normally avoids, such as the television cabinet, which contains mechanical equipment to raise and lower the television. "He said never again would he work with such mechanics," Lewis said. "He doesn't like mechanics."

What Walsh does like is to work slowly, sketching out his ideas at first in pencil or charcoal, which he follows with wood models to present to his client. "I remember vividly when he presented his ideas and models for our various commissions—they fully came to life," Bobby Taubman said when

PAGE 184 ABOVE
Joseph Walsh Studio, Eximon outdoor dining table, Connemara marble, 2016

PAGE 184 BELOW
Joseph Walsh Studio, Eximon outdoor dining table, with aluminum and cast resin extensions, 2016

PAGE 185 ABOVE
Joseph Walsh Studio, Exilumen table, Connemara marble and clear resin, 2016

PAGE 185 BELOW
Joseph Walsh Studio, Erosion side tables, travertine, 2016

he introduced Walsh at a dinner connected to LongHouse Reserve, the sculpture park and garden in East Hampton that was created by the textile designer Jack Lenor Larson, who in a coincidence further connecting Walsh to East Hampton, was an early mentor of his. The dinner honored Walsh for his contributions to design in the winter of 2020, well after Blue Dream had been completed, but the house was a vivid presence in the evening's program. Michael Lewis introduced Taubman, and then Taubman spoke about Walsh, saying he is "not just a brilliant designer, he is a technical genius and a true master craftsman." "I dine at your tables, I sit on your benches, use your door handles bent into the most contorted of shapes, and sleep in your bed—we are lucky to live in your splendor!" Bobby Taubman concluded.

Michael Lewis and the Taubmans also worked closely with Anders Ruhwald, a Danish-American artist who headed the Ceramics department at the Cranbrook Academy of Art in Bloomfield Hills. Charles Renfro had wanted all the bathroom walls in Blue Dream to curve, reflecting the general lines of the house, which meant that using conventional flat tile would be problematic. "We came up with three-millimeter-thin porcelain sheets, and Anders figured out a way to make them into a wall covering," Michael Lewis said. Ruhwald devised a pattern, different in each bathroom, which was replicated digitally to align the porcelain sheets to the unique lines and shape of each bathroom (pp. 212–13 and 216–17). In some bathrooms the lines of the pattern were undulating, in others they were angled, and in others they were almost, but not quite, rectangular, gently echoing the pattern of traditional tiles and yet strikingly new and different. Each bathroom was given its own color as well, including the bath in the guest suite, where the lines echoed German expressionism, but the color was bright yellow, as if *The Cabinet of Dr. Caligari* had been redone as a sunny children's story. All of the bathrooms were another case of using Blue Dream to celebrate the heritage of modernism and subvert it at the same time. Ruhwald also designed glass door handles for the shower enclosures as well as hooks for robes and towels, which were fabricated in collaboration with Detroit glass artist Kim Harty. But his impact on the house was not limited to practical elements. He also created several pure art pieces the Taubmans used, including a large, bright orange glazed ceramic cone, modeled after a traffic cone, that sits as a sculpture inside the front door, a sculpture in wood for the study, and a white glazed ceramic sculpture in the powder room.

Anders Ruhwald, Study for master bathroom wall covering, 2016

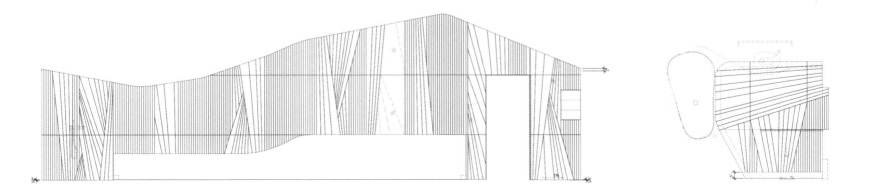

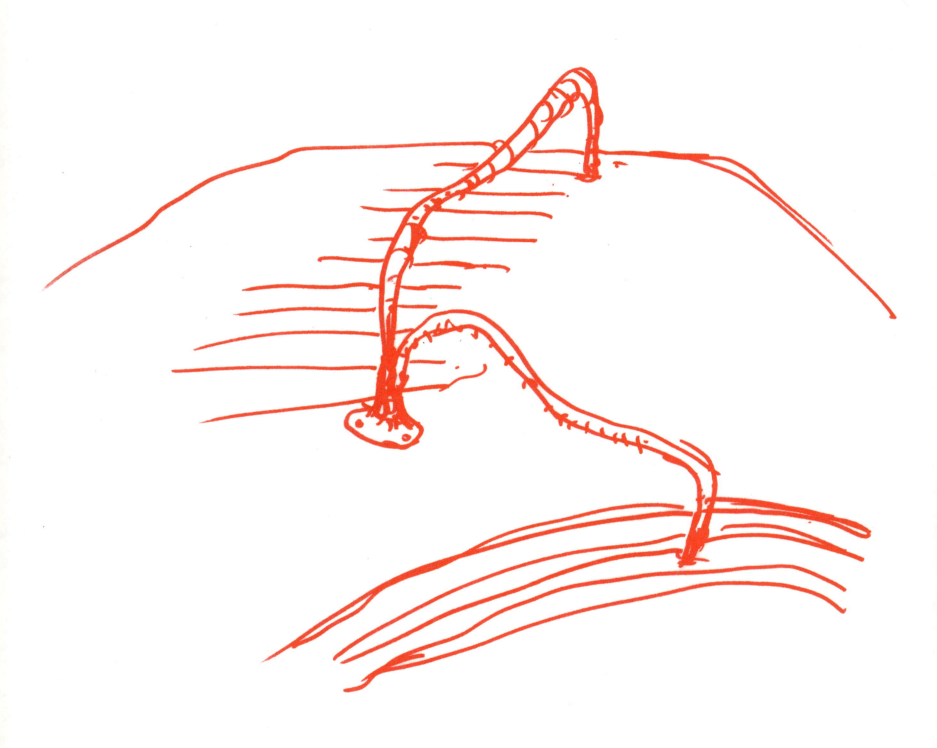

Charles Renfro, Sketch for the cast bronze handrail

Certain other elements, like the metal staircase railings, were designed by Charles Renfro and intended to be integral to the architecture. The staircase railings were not an afterthought: Renfro devoted as much time to them as to any single detail in the house. "We must have done 150 versions," Renfro said. The final version, a composition of swirling lines and sections swooping down to connect to the floor, is a dance in metal, its lines not entirely dissimilar to those of Joseph Walsh's work. Renfro wanted the railings to complement rather than interrupt the flowing lines of the mounds into which the stairs were cut. He produced version after version of the curving rail, and he became accustomed, he said, "to hearing Julie Taubman say, 'I don't know, Charles, is that as good as you can do?'—which was her way of saying she wasn't happy with it. And when she liked something, she would say 'wrap it up'." The stairs themselves were not conventionally built staircases, but steps cut into the material that formed the floors and curved upwards, becoming the mounds that enclosed the guest wing and lower bedrooms and served as the podium for the study. The floors and the interior mounds were made of plaster.

In the end, every room was a collaboration between DS+R, who shaped the space itself, and Michael Lewis and Julie Taubman, who worked jointly to select objects for each room, and then position them within it. The objects themselves are essential, and every room is a composition on its own terms. The result is a house that is filled to the brim, a modernist version of a Victorian villa in which every object is necessary and placed with precision, either to punctuate the space or to play off against the other pieces around it. It is an assemblage, and if there is one tenet of modernism that the house rejects completely, it is the notion of minimalism. It is almost baroque in its complexity, and every room is a dense composition in which the arrangement of the interiors is as complicated and as vital to the overall idea as the exterior architecture.

In this sense, Blue Dream is different from a modernist masterwork like the Farnsworth House or Fallingwater, in which the furnishings, however carefully chosen, are largely subservient to the architecture, and recede in memory before the power of the structure itself and the space it creates. The structure and space of Blue Dream are powerful, but so are the contents, and it is in the interplay between the two that the magic of the house resides. By this measure, Blue Dream recalls another great modernist masterpiece, Joseph Hoffmann's Palais Stoclet in Brussels (1905–11), in which Hoffmann orchestrated not only the Viennese Secessionist architecture, but also the collaboration of great artists like Gustav Klimt, who designed mosaic friezes, Ludwig Heinrich Jungnickel, who created murals, and Franz Metzner, who sculpted four figures for the exterior. Most of the furnishings

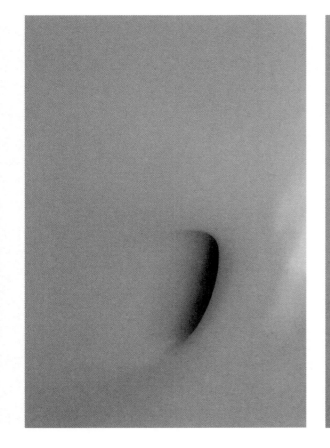
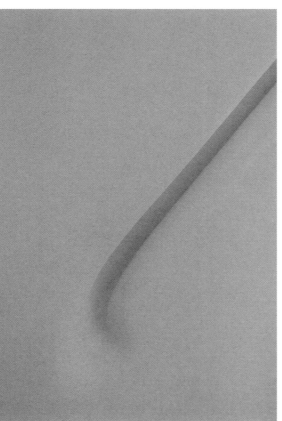

 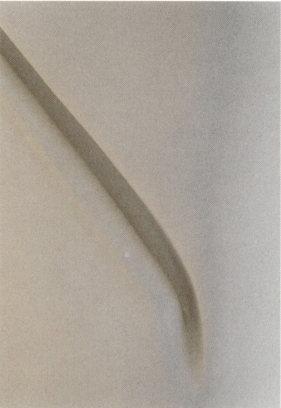 

Integrated door pulls, handrails, and stairs crafted of the same type of plaster used throughout the interior

191 *Gesamtkunstwerk* on the Atlantic Double Dunes

Charles Renfro, Sketch for the fleshy interior doors with belly button latch sets

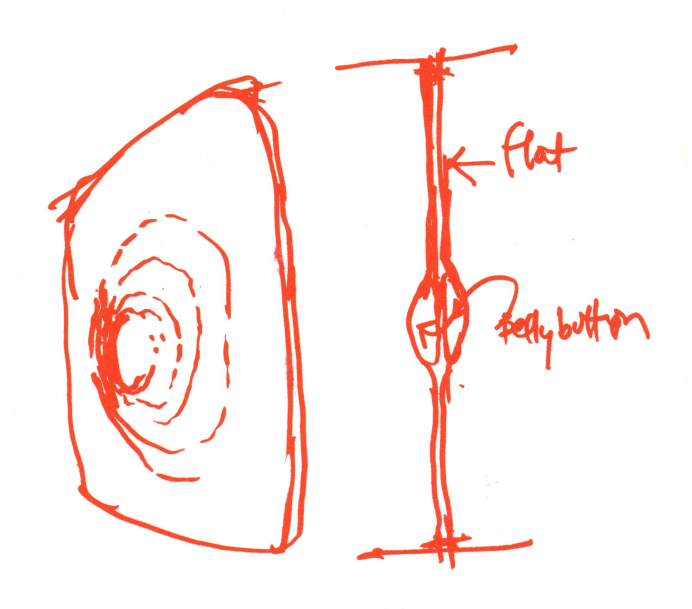

192

Mock-ups for various custom hardware details

193   *Gesamtkunstwerk* on the Atlantic Double Dunes

Charles Renfro, Plan sketch of the three-sided indoor-outdoor fire column

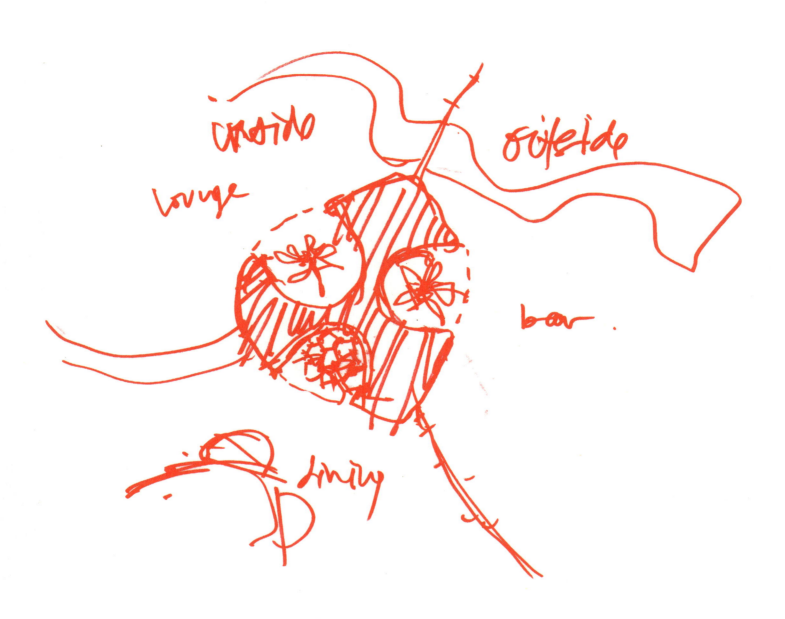

for the Palais Stoclet were designed by Hoffmann himself, which makes it different from Blue Dream, an ode to collecting as much as to commissioning, and certainly a celebration of diverse taste in which no single artist or designer controlled all, as Hoffmann had in Brussels. Yet both houses were designed with the goal of creating a *Gesamtkunstwerk*, a total work of art. As architectural historian Eduard F. Sekler wrote of Stoclet, "The house cannot be understood fully without the collection nor the collection without its splendid container; for the Stoclets, both demanded a continuous adherence to self-imposed, exacting standards."

So, too, with Blue Dream: the collection and its container are inseparable, and both owed a debt to the determination and intellectual rigor of the clients. Not least of Blue Dream's accomplishments is to have achieved this not with a small handful of designers all connected to a single movement, as Hoffmann did with his Vienna Secession colleagues, but to have crafted a *Gesamtkunstwerk* with the far more diverse cadre of artists, designers, and craftspeople that Michael Lewis and Julie Taubman assembled for this house.

It works, to say it again, because of the skill with which each room has been composed. The guest room, for example, is a voluptuous cave, a fully conceived space in which the architecture and the objects within it form a coherent whole, the placement of every light fixture and every piece of furniture becoming a response to every line of the architecture (pp. 210–11). Everything is intentional, and even the smallest object is a part of a larger composition: In the living room (pp. 160–61), the high arc of Nanda Vigo's *Golden Gate Lamp*, a six-and-a-half-foot-long arc of chrome, plays off beautifully against the lines of the ceiling and the glass walls, its sleek form deferring to Yin Xiuzhen's bright and powerful *Life Raft* beside it; and then,

LEFT
Basalt columns

RIGHT
Model of fireplace inspired by the basalt columns

on the other side of *Life Raft*, the active shape of Misha Kahn's sculptural lamp, *A Sentinel of Inevitability*, a playful, eight-foot-high composition in resin, paint, copper, and silk, an ideal counterpoint to the Nanda. However different these two pieces are, both are punctuation marks in the space: neither dominates the room nor interrupts the view. Nearby is an expansive *Prosciutto* sofa in white leather by Marc Newson, conventional only by comparison to *Life Raft*, and his *Hollow Core Table* of glass and marble; Humberto and Fernando Campana's *Pirarucu* sofa, made of leather and bamboo; Joris Laarman's *Bone Armchair*, made of white Carrara marble powder and resin, which Julie Taubman purchased from Dennis Freedman; and Nacho Carbonell's *Table Cocoon 5*, a metal-frame console table fitted with crushed metal mesh sculpture that is also a lamp. Together, all of these pieces make up a seating area in which solid and void, heavy and light, open and enclosed, light and dark, play off against one another and against the space.

Julie Taubman's wide-ranging collections set the tone, embracing and critiquing modernism at the same time, in ways that are sometimes wry, often surreal, and almost without exception, beautiful. That ensured that there would be a consistency of vision in Blue Dream, for all the diversity of design voices that the Taubmans collected and commissioned. But just as critical was Michael Lewis. His sensitivity not just to Julie's, eye but also to the architecture of DS+R, and his determination to use interior design to support rather than undermine the architecture, was vital to the assemblage of every room in the house. Powerful architecture can easily overwhelm what is placed in it; the history of modern architecture is filled with houses that look better empty than full, and that are memorable as structures more than as containers for the lives lived within them. Michael Lewis's great accomplishment was to balance Julie Taubman's eye and DS+R's architecture, and to bring them into harmony in Blue Dream.

MOVING TOWARD COMPLETION

That getting Blue Dream built would be difficult surprised no one, although the issues surrounding the roof structure and exterior panels, and the delays it brought, turned out to be greater than anyone on the design team had anticipated. Ed Bulgin's calm demeanor—a surfer and practitioner of meditation, he seemed always to maintain an even keel—made a huge difference during tense periods. He saw himself not only as a technician searching for solutions, but also as a kind of coach whose objective was to keep his team members motivated. Bulgin's goal was to make every construction worker feel that it was a privilege to play a role in the building of Blue Dream. "My position was to convince the plumber that this was the Olympics of construction," Bulgin said. "I was amazed at the dedication of the people who worked here." Bulgin and his chief deputy for the project, David Currie, generally tried to make a point of not challenging the validity of DS+R's designs from an architectural standpoint; they would question them only where they saw issues of practicality or buildability, but they never tried to substitute their own design judgment for DS+R's. That, in turn, earned the architects' respect, and made them more comfortable when Bulgin or Currie did object to specific elements of the design. Ed Bulgin was the one figure whom Charles Renfro, Michael Lewis, and Bobby Taubman would all describe as indispensable. "Without Bulgin it couldn't have been done," Lewis said.

The year 2015 was an especially challenging one for the Taubman family, as they navigated not only the ongoing problems of construction (by then the assembly of fiberglass panels was underway), but also the loss of Alfred Taubman, who died at 91 in April. Shortly thereafter, Julie Taubman was diagnosed with advanced breast cancer in June. Initially, she did not share the news beyond the family, but later that year, Bobby Taubman saw Charles Renfro in Los Angeles at the opening of The Broad, and told him about her illness. Renfro had grown close to Julie by then, and was deeply shaken by the news. At that point the house was moving toward a completion date in late 2016, but the news of Julie's cancer led to an acceleration of the timetable. It was agreed that there would be no further changes to the design, and that the house would be made ready for occupancy by June of 2016 so that the Taubmans could enjoy a summer on the dunes.

Two critical elements could not be completed in time. Renfro's stair railings, which were still being fabricated, and the front door, a custom design by DS+R which was not even conceived until long after construction had started. Early in the design process, Julie had said she wanted the house to have an unusual front door. "It should be strange and weird and totally out of proportion," she said to the architects. Initially, DS+R had proposed a metal door in a bulging shape so that it would look more like an abstract sculpture than a flat door panel. Their three-dimensional printer produced a model of the design with thin curving lines, which Michael Lewis thought resembled a fingerprint. That, in turn, gave Lewis an idea: what if the door were designed to look like a huge fingerprint? Julie proposed taking it further, making it not a generic fingerprint, but a reproduction of her own actual thumbprint on one side, and Bobby's on the other. It was, everyone agreed, the right way to create a one-of-a-kind door that would be suitable for the house. But it would take some time for Ed Bulgin to figure out how to get it made.

Both the door and the stair railings were fabricated out of white bronze, a material that Renfro and Julie settled on as the only metal that seemed both warm and possessed of sufficient depth and gravitas. Aluminum felt too light, stainless steel too shiny, raw steel too industrial. With a size and weight more like the door to a bank vault, the door was a remarkable way to give what was already a highly personal house an even more personal mark, the swirling pattern of thumbprints in bas-relief softly echoing the curving lines

Study models for the front door

Moving toward completion

Charles Renfro, Sketch of the fat front door with integrated pull

LEFT
Original 3D digital print suggesting fingerprint ridges

RIGHT
Fabrication and installation of final fat fingerprint front door

Moving toward completion

of the house itself. The enormous piece was less a custom-made door than a two-sided piece of sculpture that would be hung and balanced so that it could easily swing open. After a long search for fabricators, Ed Bulgin arranged for the door and the stair railings to be crafted by Polich Tallix, the celebrated sculpture foundry in upstate New York which had fabricated work for Louise Bourgeois, Joel Shapiro, Jeff Koons, and other artists. But the foundry could not meet the summer 2016 deadline, so Bulgin made a temporary door to fit the enormous opening left for the thumbprint door, and installed temporary stair railings so that the local building inspector would grant the Taubmans a certificate of occupancy that allowed them to move in.

Even with the accelerated timetable, there were delays. The biggest delay involved reworking the sunken bathtub in the master suite, an elaborate, curved design roughly in the shape of an amoeba, carefully positioned to allow an occupant of the tub to gaze upward through a skylight. Julie Taubman loved the shape, but found the terrazzo surface more monochromatic than what she had hoped for. She came up with the notion of enlivening the tub by setting into the terrazzo several pieces of a brightly patterned marble with elements of blue and green that had been carved into sinks and a vanity counter in the bathroom, which Holly Deichmann and Michael Lewis then placed like sculptural elements within the curvilinear form of the tub. The result, if not the extra time it took to achieve it, pleased everyone.

Palladiana terrazzo tub during fabrication

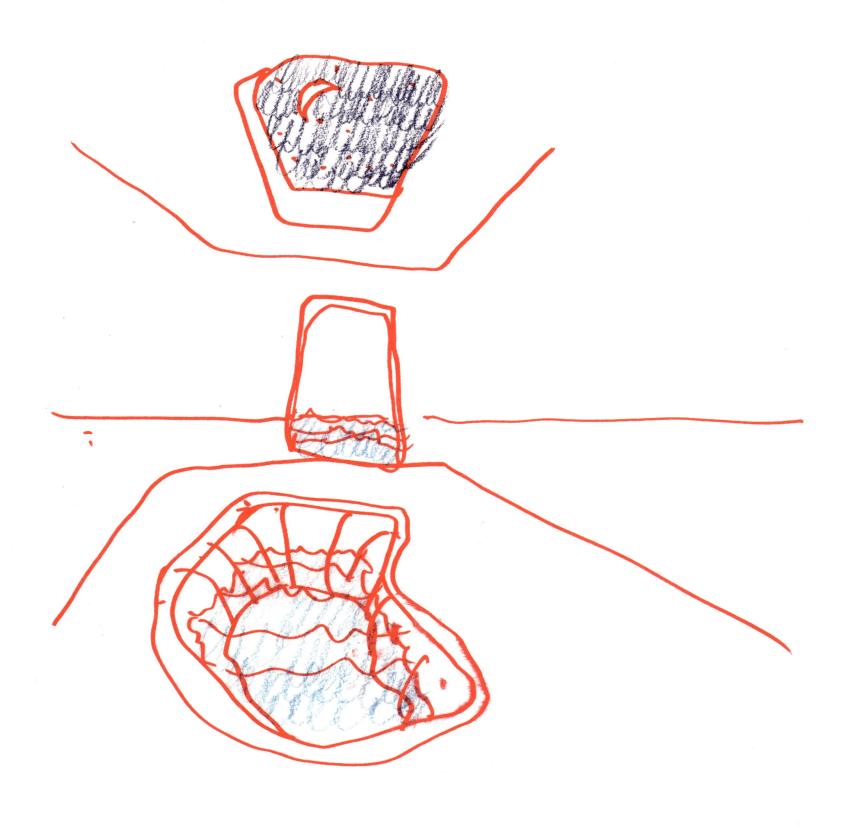

Charles Renfro, Sketch of portals for viewing the ocean and the sky from the tub

By August of 2016, most of the interior elements were in place. So were several final pieces of the exterior, including an extraordinary gate that opened in the manner of a drawbridge, another engineering challenge that Ed Bulgin figured out how to meet. Julie had seen a simple metal chain link gate in an airport that opened upwards, and said she much preferred the way it worked to a conventional gate that swung or slid open. The airport gate was light and porous, however, allowing wind to move through it, while Blue Dream's vertical pivot lift gate would need to be solid to provide privacy, and it had to be crafted of steel and wood strong enough to withstand hurricane-force winds. All of this would make it too heavy to use the simple mechanism that operated the chain link gate at the airport. Bulgin had to engineer a system more suited to a vertical lift bridge than the entry to an estate. Bulgin's research led him to gate engineering for military installations, such as those used in war zones.

The gate, which has the name of the house carved into the wood, leads into a curving driveway that meanders through a dune-like landscape toward the house. The site plan is carefully choreographed to work along with the architecture, revealing both the house and the ocean gradually. Neither is visible at first; the house slowly comes into view after the driveway bends to the right, then curves left, DS+R's billowing shape playing off against the

Upward-pivoting entry gate

surrounding dunes. But the ocean is kept hidden, tantalizingly near but not revealed until you go through the door of the house and up a few steps to the main living area and the expanse of water becomes visible through the expanse of glass.

Much of the site planning was done by Michael Boucher, a distinguished landscape architect based in Freeport, Maine, whose practice has long focused on the relationship of landscape to contemporary architecture. Boucher, who had previously worked with Liz Diller on some of her projects, joined the team at Diller's suggestion not long after DS+R were hired. As Michael Lewis had done with the interiors, Boucher saw his role as complementing the architecture of the house, not competing with it, and his designs gracefully complemented DS+R's work on the exterior as Lewis's did on the interior. Boucher was well aware of the unusual nature of the Atlantic Double Dunes Preserve that the Taubman property faced, and set out to reflect both its native vegetation and its linear rhythms.

He wanted the property to subtly echo the landscape of the entire region, evolving in stages into a seascape as it moved south toward the ocean. Boucher placed groves of evergreens on the northernmost part of the site just inside the gate to reflect the native landscape of eastern Long Island, and placed a small lawn area—the only one on the property—as a gentle, ironic nod to the traditional East Hampton estates that Blue Dream in every other way bore little resemblance to. He reshaped the sections of the property closest to the house into dunes that gently echoed the curves of the house and planted them with high, flowing sea grasses. Throughout the property, the landscape retained the undulating lines of the actual dunes the house faced. Boucher knew from the beginning that this was not a property for long *allées* of trees or decorative shrubs or expansive lawns, though formal elements like these were hardly his style anyway.

Early in the design process, DS+R talked often about how they had wanted the form of the house to echo the lines of the dunes. It does, although it is impossible to know how much this can be attributed to the architects' conscious wish to evoke the image of the dunes and how much it comes their longtime predilection for certain shapes. But if it is difficult to say with

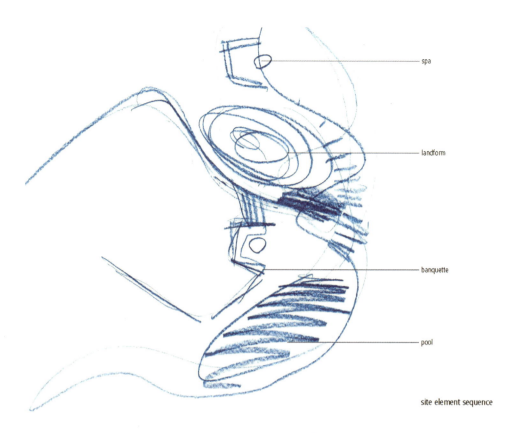

site element sequence

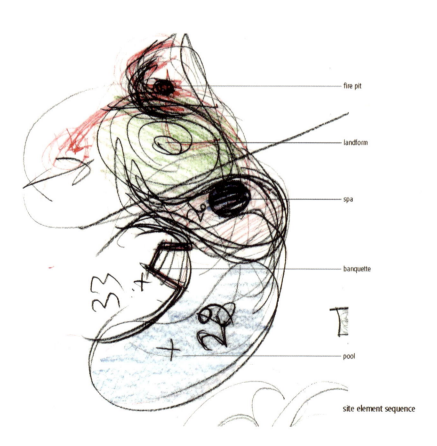

site element sequence

OPPOSITE

A meandering and flexible wooden footpath leads from Blue Dream to a bridge across the rare ecological zone of the double dunes. The 450-foot path made of decking slats spaced an inch apart and bound together with nylon rope rests lightly on the ground. Extending 150 feet from the end of the footpath, the bridge, also constructed of wood decking and supported on four-by-four posts, hovers four to six feet over the dunes before steps descend to the beach, a drop of about ten feet depending on seasonal erosion levels.

ABOVE AND BELOW
Michael Boucher, Conceptual spa terrace studies, January 2011

Moving toward completion

Michael Boucher, Site plan and grading study, prior to the garage, January 2011

Michael Boucher, Overall site plan including the double dunes, December 2010

certainty how much the house echoes the dunes, thanks to Michael Boucher, it is clear that the dunes echo the house, and that the architecture and the landscape reinforce one another other. Boucher has responded to DS+R's architecture with a modernist essay in dunescape.

Ed Bulgin also oversaw a large and complex secondary structure designed by DS+R to contain a garage and gymnasium. It was set to the north of the main house, burrowed into an artificial dune designed by Michael Boucher as a way to hide the garage and gym and to extend the undulating form of the dunes further inland across the property. The gym, set behind a facade of glass framed by an arc of concrete, faces an adjacent tennis court. Insofar as it can be seen as a bold exercise in modernism, it is consistent with the rest of the house; from another standpoint, however, it is more conventional, since its facade is symmetrical and framed in concrete, the very material that proved unworkable for the house itself. But its differences from the main house are also a form of deference: to have created a miniature copy of Blue Dream as a gym or a garage would have trivialized the house and compromised its essential quality, uniqueness. The gym structure is a thing unto itself, complementing the house, but not replicating it.

BELOW
Michael Boucher, Double-sided mound scheme, December 2010

OPPOSITE
Michael Boucher, Key plan for renderings of the dunes illustrated in section, December 2010

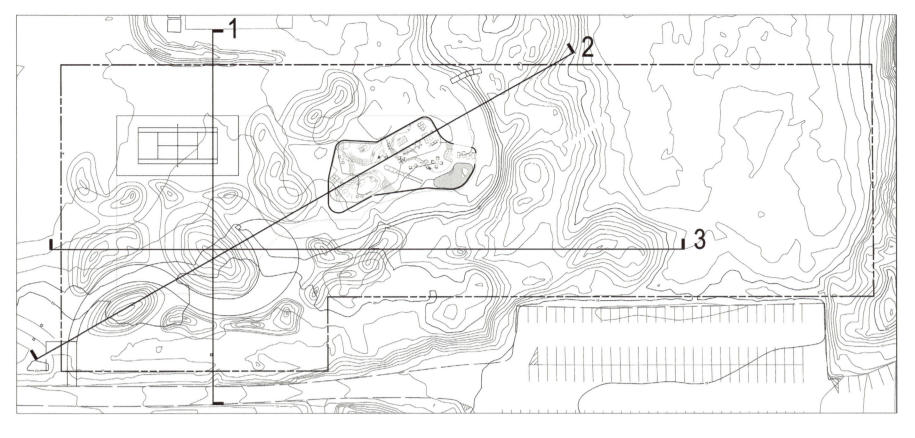

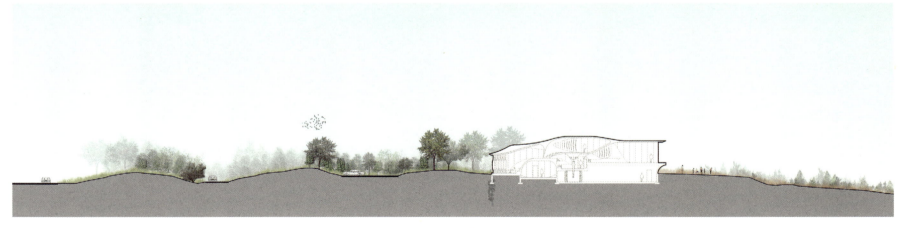

Julie Taubman welcomed friends to the house for the rest of that first summer, including Liz Diller, Ric Scofidio, and Charles Renfro, who arrived for an August visit bearing a gift: a vase they had chosen to complete the composition of the powder room, whose walls were lined with black plaster. Julie hosted a celebratory outdoor dinner that same month, filling every seat at Joseph Walsh's extended, curving outdoor dining table. At Thanksgiving, Julie and Bobby invited the rest of the Taubman family and the Reyes family to celebrate the holiday at Blue Dream, by which time the front door and stair railings had been installed and the house was, for all intents and purposes, complete. She and Bobby spent much of the following summer in East Hampton and returned to the house as often as they could manage while she underwent further cancer treatment near her home in Michigan. She had one more summer at Blue Dream, and then passed away at her home in Bloomfield Hills in January 2018. Bobby Taubman and his children have continued to occupy the house, and they maintain it precisely as Julie envisioned it.

Vaulted concrete viewing pavilion, gym, and garage embedded in the dune bordering the tennis court

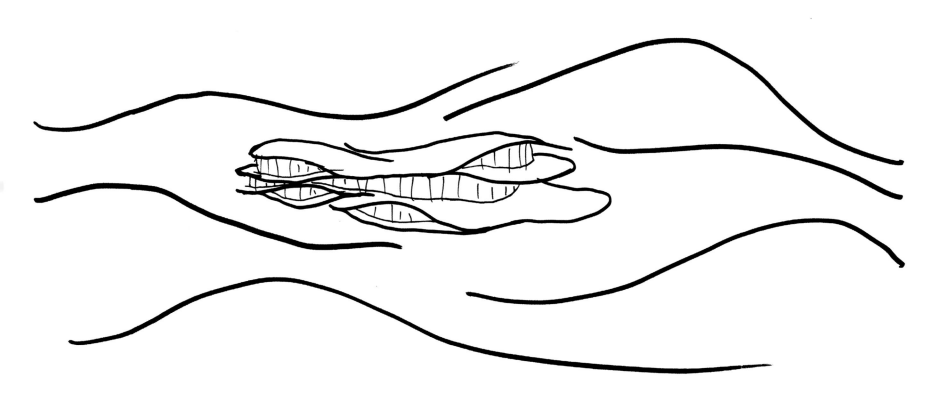

MAKING MODERNISM NEW AGAIN

What is the significance of a house like Blue Dream? It is not, after all, a model. It does not represent a prototype for other houses. It is a unique object, one that builds on the history of avant-garde art and architecture on Eastern Long Island, and it emerges out of a desire to renew and re-energize that history, to make it new once again. Radical design that questions the *status quo* has a history that is uneven, at best, in the Hamptons in the 21st century, as it is in most communities of substantial means. It is no surprise that Blue Dream's newly built neighbors are mostly traditional houses. Even the sleek and sumptuous houses of glass and wood that in recent years have been interspersed with the neo-traditional mansions in the Hamptons and marketed by real estate agents as 'modern' could be considered to represent an equally traditional attitude, since now, in the 21st century, they too evoke a kind of historical style, almost as venerable a part of the Hamptons heritage, in its way, as the Shingle Style. These new and grand modernist villas, seductive and luxurious though they are, do not represent invention, but rather an acceptance of established precedent, and the evolution of modernism into a historic style.

Blue Dream is something else: for all the luxury that it too represents, and for all that it is, in the end, a grand oceanfront villa more than one of the light modernist pavilions of the postwar era, it is nevertheless a genuine attempt to re-assert the notion of a more radical architectural possibility, the notion that modernism is energized by reinvention and change, and that this is more deeply woven into the DNA of modern architecture than luxury and grandeur. Blue Dream is like nothing that has come before it, and that, in and of itself, ties it more closely than anything built in the Hamptons in more than a generation to the great desire of modernism, the quest, to paraphrase Ezra Pound, to forever make it new.

Invention and radical change, are not, in and of themselves, essential to the making of good architecture, and every building, every house, does not have to represent cutting-edge creativity. Few buildings are good enough to be meaningful reinventions, and civilized architecture that gently follows precedent frequently serves us as well as anything else. But every so often,

PAGE 260
Charles Renfro, The Dunes, concept sketch

a combination of extraordinary architect and extraordinary client yields a work that is different from anything that has been built before, a result that shifts the architectural needle, however slightly, and creates an object of potent visual and emotional power. So it was with the combination of Frank Lloyd Wright and the Kaufmanns that brought forth Fallingwater, with Le Corbusier and the Savoyes that led to the Villa Savoye, and even the combustible, troubled relationship between Mies van der Rohe and Edith Farnsworth that created the Farnsworth House.

Behind every notable house—and many un-notable ones—is the story of a client as much as an architect, the story of how they joined together to create something that neither party could have done on its own. This is particularly true in the case of Blue Dream. The clients began with a love of the ocean, a love of modernism, the idea of making it new, and they sought a house that would weave these things together. It embraces paradox, since it is an ode to collecting, which is fundamentally conservative, and to designing in a new way, which is fundamentally radical. It is about technology, it is about traditional craft, it is about the land, and it is about objects. It is both a private meditation and a public statement. Time will judge whether Blue Dream belongs in the group of extraordinary, one-of-a-kind houses that are recorded in the annals of architectural history. Many houses have aspired to iconic status, and few that have attained it.

Regardless, Blue Dream is not a house for anyone other than Julie and Robert Taubman; it is not a model for anything else. But, to say it again, for a house to be a lasting work of architecture it does not have to be a model; it can be an aesthetic statement, a structural experiment, a sculptural event, a re-evaluation of history, an interpretation of a time—any of these things, or perhaps all of them—more than it is a prototype for others to follow. The world has one Fallingwater, one Villa Savoye, one Edith Farnsworth House—or, going back much farther in history, one Villa Rotunda, one Monticello, one Sir John Soane's Museum, the latter two of which, like Blue Dream, emerged out of a collector's passion as much as an architect's instincts (although in the case of both Monticello and the Soane Museum, the collector, the client, and the architect were one and the same person). And to return to the 20th century, there is only one Palais Stoclet, which in some ways is an even better comparison to Blue Dream, since there, as at Blue Dream, enlightened clients commissioned architecture, furniture design, and art as a total work of art, a *Gesamptkunstwerk*, and the result was an ornate and complex interior inseparable from a striking and new exterior that looked like nothing that had ever been built before.

The world has no need to replicate any of these houses, because what we learn from them is not to see them as prototypes; each offers us a certain way of seeing, a certain way of shaping space and form, and takes it as far as it can go. To think of it as indicating a direction to follow would only be to encourage weak echoes of it, not to build on its ideas. Far better to see each of these one-of-a-kind houses as an act of aesthetic brilliance, as a new way of making space and form that will cause the rest of us to experience the world a little more intensely. And we can see each of them also as a window into certain peoples' lives, and how in each case architects sought a unique way of expressing the aspirations of those lives. A house that is also a great work of architecture, a place that is at once a place to live and a work of art, tells us much about a particular way of life, but that does not mean we need to live that same life to appreciate it, or to learn from it—or to share in the joy that its forms, swirling over the dunes, can bring.

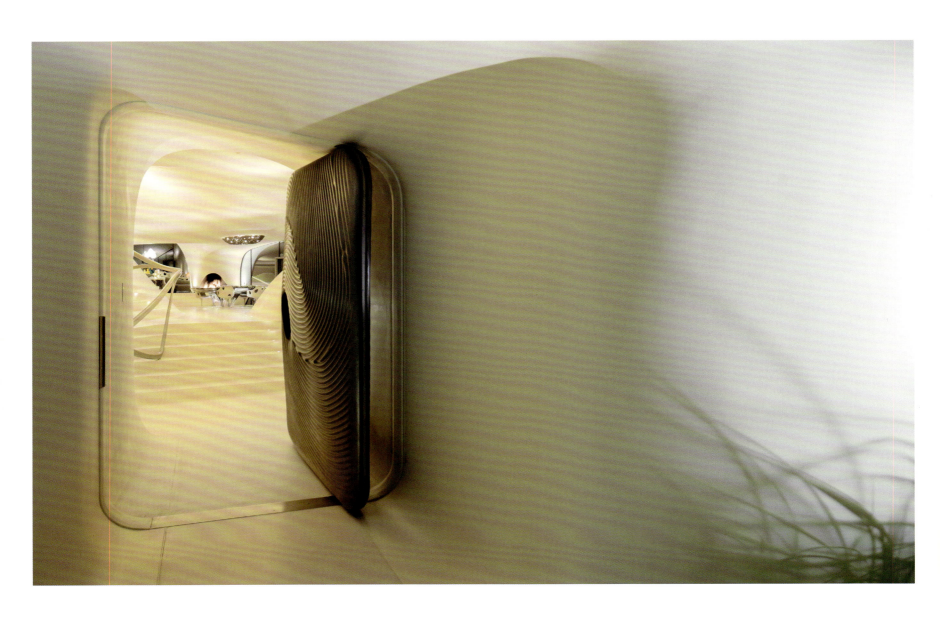

A NOTE FROM THE AUTHOR

Most architectural history is written from the standpoint of architects—what was he or she trying to do in the design of a particular building, how did it come into being, how did it relate to the development of their career, what is its place in the larger arc of history, and so forth. While I hope that this book addresses these questions, it is also an attempt to look at the making of an important work of architecture in terms of the interplay between the clients who commissioned it, the architects who designed it, and the people who built it. Clients are essential to any building project, of course, but in the case of a commercial building the client is often the corporation that initiates the project and pays the bills, and the people who will use the building are, in effect, the client's customers. The client is not the user, in the same way that the client is not the user in a hospital, a school, a courthouse, or an airport.

But a private house is different. The client is the user; the client, and only the client, is the person or the couple or the family for whom the design is made, and it has no other reason for being. The person who pays for it is the person who will live with it, who will love it or be frustrated by it—or perhaps some of both—and will have a relationship to its architect that is far more intimate than the one that exists with any other kind of building project. (Not for nothing do many architects who specialize in houses sometimes think of themselves as akin to family therapists.)

When both the client and the architect have extraordinary ambitions, and when the clients are as knowledgeable and passionate about modern design as Julie and Robert Taubman, and the architects as committed to finding a new set of forms to express beauty and enhance living as Liz Diller, Ric Scofidio, Charles Renfro, and Holly Deichmann, it is impossible not to tell the story of what resulted as a chronicle of the dynamic between client and architect. The ambitions of the Taubmans drove the architects as well as all the other designers who played a role in the realization of this house; the ambitions of the architects and designers drove the Taubmans. They occasionally irritated one another, but more often they inspired one another to produce a work that went beyond what most of them had done before. That is the story of Blue Dream.

Long ago, when Julie and Bobby Taubman purchased their property in East Hampton, we spoke about the Taubmans' hopes for their house, and I was one of the many people Julie consulted in her initial search for an architect.

Later, when the Diller Scofidio + Renfro house was under construction, the Taubmans spoke about their desire to have the house chronicled in book form rather than published in a magazine and asked if I would be interested in writing it. I agreed, but as the house neared completion, other projects intervened; then Julie Taubman's illness delayed the development of this book still further. Sadly, her death prevented us from having the extended conversations about the house that we both had hoped for, but we had many casual discussions about it before her illness, and I had a clear understanding of her design sensibility as well as how it shaped her vision for this house.

At a late point in Julie's illness, Bobby Taubman invited me to Michigan to visit with her in the hope that a renewed conversation about the house would be a pleasing thing for her. It would surely have been pleasing for me, but alas, her condition took a turn for the worse in the days just before the trip, and the visit never took place. But my first thanks must go to Julie, both for imagining Blue Dream in the first place, and for those early conversations that helped me to understand her aspirations.

Some months after Julie's death in 2018, Bobby Taubman was back in touch to say that he wanted the project to move forward, and it did. He has been an extraordinary partner in this project: always available, articulate about both the house and Julie's role in it, candid about recalling the moments of stress, and exuberant about the pleasures of the house. He has been continually supportive of the idea of telling the entire story of Blue Dream and how it came to be. My gratitude to Bobby Taubman is immense.

I am also grateful to the Taubmans for their decision to invite Iwan Baan, one of the greatest architectural photographers not just of our time, but of any time, to document the house. It is an honor to have my words accompany his serene and majestic images.

Liz Diller, Ric Scofidio, and Charles Renfro, and their talented colleague Holly Deichmann have been gracious, enthusiastic, and hard-working on behalf of this project: like Bobby Taubman, they have been available, candid, and a pleasure to work with, and I am particularly indebted to both Charles and Holly for extended conversations. I am also grateful to their former colleague Quang Truon for discussing with me his role in the development of the complex roof structure. Of course, the house could not have come into being without all of these people, but it is important to state that neither could this book have come to be without their warm and generous cooperation.

Lorraine Wild is a designer of great skill who understands both the making of books and the making of architecture as well as anyone; moreover, she is a longtime friend of Julie Taubman and collaborated with Julie on many projects, including designing Julie's magnificent book of photographs of Detroit and the graphic identity of the Museum of Contemporary Art Detroit (MOCAD). Lorraine, like I, had watched Blue Dream take shape since the beginning, and it has been both a pleasure and a privilege to work with her on this project.

Lorraine, in turn, brought Denise Bratton to the project as editor, and also to research historical material. She handled a multitude of other tasks with grace, skill, and sensitivity. I owe Denise sincere thanks.

Over the course of research, I had many conversations with Michael Lewis, who not only graciously responded to every question about his work and his role in the realization of the house but also offered wise counsel on numerous other matters related to the house. Dennis Freedman welcomed me to his house in East Hampton for a wonderful talk about Julie's collecting and their shared sensibilities. Brad Dunning talked with me about his early role as an advisor to Julie. Late in the project, I had stimulating conversations with Joseph Walsh about his work and his philosophy of craft and design. Michael Boucher generously discussed the role of landscape played in this project. I owe a very special thanks to Ed Bulgin, with whom I had a long, warm, and meaningful conversation one spring morning in the living room of an otherwise empty Blue Dream, a conversation that was enormously helpful to the completion of this book. It is no surprise that so many people connected with Blue Dream feel that without Ed, the house could not have been built.

Tom Phifer was gracious in talking with me about what was, understandably, a difficult moment in his impressive career. Peter Gluck, another architect whose design the Taubmans ultimately chose not to build, generously shared with us information about the origins of his design, and also assisted us with our search for archival images.

My thanks to Daniela Hellmich for her indispensable assistance with archival material. Olger Araya, who manages Blue Dream for the Taubmans, has been consistently helpful, as has Bina Reid.

As I said at the beginning of this book, this is the story of clients as much as architects, and let me end with another word about Bobby Taubman. He and Julie approached the building of their house with high aspirations, which were realized. His commitment to this book indicated a wish that it be equally ambitious. I am hopeful that the book about Blue Dream achieves the same high standard as the house that inspired it.

Paul Goldberger
New York, January 2023

DILLER SCOFIDIO + RENFRO STUDIO AND BLUE DREAM CONSULTANTS

Charles Renfro, Partner in Charge
Liz Diller, *Partner*
Ric Scofidio, *Partner*
Ben Gilmartin, *Partner*

Holly Deichmann, *Associate Principal + Project Director*
Quang Truong, *Project Architect*
Bryce Suite, *Associate + Project Architect*
Michael Etzel, *Senior Associate, Concept Designer*
Chris Andreacola
Óskar Arnórsson
Alice Chai
Thomas Carruthers
Ann Coombs
Amber Foo
Alina Gorokhova
Garrick Jones
Trevor Lamphier
Mark Morris
Kevin Murray
Stefano Paiocchi
Andrés Oyaga Loewy
Jorge Pereira
Haruka Saito

Consultants
Lauri Etela, Client Representative
Daniel Sesil, LERA Consulting Structural Engineers, New York City
David Kendall, Optima Projects, Ltd., Lymington, England, FRP Structural Engineer
Polise Consulting Engineers, P.C., New York City, Mechanical, Electrical, and Plumbing Engineers
Michael Boucher, Landscape Architecture (MBLA), Freeport, Maine
Isometrix Lighting + Design, London, England, Lighting Designer
D.B. Bennett, Consulting Engineer, East Hampton, New York, Civil Engineer
Saskas Surveying Company, P.C., East Hampton, New York, Surveyor
Construction Specifications, Inc., Morganville, New Jersey, Specifications Consultant
Michael Paul Lewis, Interior Designer, New York and Paris
Bulgin & Associates, Inc., Southampton, New York, General Contractor
Erik Bruce, Inc., Brooklyn, New York, Drapery Consultant

Specialty Fabricators and General Contractor Consultants
Janicki Industries, Sedro-Woolley, Washington, FRP Roof
Eckersley O'Callaghan, New York City, Facade Engineering
UAP + Polich Tallix, Fine Art Foundry (Urban Art Projects), Rock Tavern, New York, Bronze Foundry
John Tibett, Precsion Stone, Inc., Westbury, New York, Terrazzo tub installation
Alberto Quiros, TQ Mason House, Inc., Hampton Bays, Marius Aurenti Interior wall and floor plaster
Tim Hayes Plastering, Inc., Mastic Beach, New York, Ceiling and Marmarino plaster
Kotronis Consulting LLC, New York City, 3D Modeling

CONTRIBUTORS

Paul Goldberger
Paul Goldberger, whom the *Huffington Post* has called "the leading figure in architecture criticism," is now a Contributing Editor at *Vanity Fair*. From 1997 through 2011 he served as the Architecture Critic for *The New Yorker*, where he wrote the magazine's celebrated "Sky Line" column. He also holds the Joseph Urban Chair in Design and Architecture at The New School in New York City. He was formerly Dean of the Parsons School of Design, a division of The New School. Goldberger began his career at The New York Times, where in 1984 his architecture criticism was awarded the Pulitzer Prize for Distinguished Criticism, the highest award in journalism.

Iwan Baan
Dutch photographer Iwan Baan is known primarily for images that narrate the life and interactions that occur within architecture. With no formal training in architecture, his perspective mirrors the questions and perspectives of the everyday individuals who give meaning and context to the architecture and spaces that surround us, and this artistic approach has given matters of architecture an approachable and accessible voice. Architects turn to Baan to give their work a sense of place and narrative within their environments.

IMAGE CREDITS

All images © Diller Scofidio + Renfro: pp. 95, 96, Courtesy Diller + Scofidio; pp. 99–103, 106, 113, 130, 131, 133 below, 136, 138, 140–152, 193, 195, 235, 237 left and upper two images on right, 238, Courtesy Diller Scofidio + Renfro; pp. 188, 192, 194, 236, 239, 260, Courtesy Charles Renfro, Diller Scofidio + Renfro

All photographs © Iwan Baan: pp. 2–12, 16, 21–31, 45–55, 81–92, 117–128, 153–176, 190–191, 197–232, 240, 242, 248–259, 265–272, 278, 280

pp. 1 and 180: Courtesy Green Dragon Office, Los Angeles

p. 15: Courtesy Katherine Bernhardt and Karma, *Diller Scofidio + Renfro, Amagansett*, 2017, published in *Houses* (New York: Katherine Bernhardt and Karma, 2018)

p. 32: Courtesy Osborne & McGowan, P.C., East Hampton, Long Island, New York

p. 34: Courtesy Alden B. Dow Archives, Midland, Michigan

p. 36: Photo © Kathleen Galligan, USA TODAY NETWORK

p. 37: Above, photo © Library of Congress, Prints & Photographs Division, Balthazar Korab Collection, LC-DIG-krb-00713; below, left and right, photo © Ezra Stoller/ESTO

p. 38: Courtesy Cranbrook Center for Collections Research and Michigan State Historic Preservation Office, photo © James Haefner

pp. 39, 104, 139: Courtesy Lorraine Wild, Green Dragon Office, Los Angeles

p. 40: Left, Photo © Tim Street-Porter, right, Julius Shulman Photography Archive, photo © J. Paul Getty Trust, Getty Research Institute, Los Angeles (2004.R.10)

p. 41: Upper left, lower right, Jacques Couëlle, photos © Gilbert Luigi; lower left, upper right, photos © E. Van der Veen and P. Toussaint

p. 42: Photo © James Haefner, Detroit, Michigan

p. 43: Above, Photo © David Erickson, Erickson Studio, Milwaukee, Wisconsin; below, © RoadsideArchitecture.com

p. 56: Photo © Ezra Stoller/ESTO

p. 58: Courtesy Fondazione Nivola, Orani, Sardinia

p. 59: Left, Photo © Estate of Barney Rosset; right, Courtesy JC Raulston Arboretum, North Carolina State University, Raleigh, North Carolina, © JC Raulston Arboretum

p. 60: Left, Courtesy Byron Company (93.1.1.10108), Museum of the City of New York; right, photo © Ezra Stoller/ESTO

p. 61: Above, Published in Frances Miller, *More About Tanty* (Sag Harbor, NY: Sandbox Press, 1980), photo © Miller Family Archive; center, photo © Avery Architectural and Fine Arts Library, Columbia University, New York; below, photo © Ezra Stoller/ESTO

p. 62: Left, Courtesy East Hampton Library Digital Long Island Collection, photo © Estate of Harvey A. Weber; right, photo © Mainspring Archive: The Andrew Geller Collection

p. 63: Photo © 1991 Hans Namuth Estate, Courtesy Center for Creative Photography, University of Arizona, Tucson, Arizona

p. 64: Above and below left, photo © Ezra Stoller/ESTO; below right, Courtesy East Hampton Library Digital Long Island Collection, photo © Estate of Harvey A. Weber

p. 65: Left and right, Courtesy 2023 Austrian Frederick and Lillian Kiesler Private Foundation, Vienna, Austria

p. 66: Above and below, photos © Norman McGrath/ESTO

p. 67: Courtesy Pratt Institute School of Information On-Site Archives and Special Collections, photo © Bill Maris

p. 69: Above, East Hampton Library Digital Long Island Collection, photo © Estate of Harvey A. Weber; below, photo © William Waldron

p. 70: Left, Photo © Ezra Stoller/ESTO; right, photo © Norman McGrath/ESTO

pp. 73–75: Courtesy Thomas Phifer & Partners

p. 77: Courtesy Preston T. Phillips, photo © Preston T. Phillips, Architect

pp. 78–80: Courtesy Peter L. Gluck, photo © Gluck+

pp. 111: Above, Courtesy LERA; below, Courtesy Dan Sesil, LERA

pp. 112: Courtesy Dan Sesil, LERA

pp. 114–115: Courtesy LERA

p. 133: Above, Courtesy Diller Scofidio + Renfro and LERA

p. 179: Courtesy Darcy Miro, photo © Darcy Miro, Brooklyn, New York

p. 182: Left and right, Courtesy Chris Schanck Studio, Detroit, Michigan

p. 183: Left and right, Courtesy Joseph Walsh Studio, Fartha, County Cork, Ireland

pp. 184–85: Courtesy Joseph Walsh Studio, Fartha, County Cork, Ireland, photos © James Harris, London, England

p. 187: Courtesy Anders Ruhwald Studio, Chicago, Illinois / Detroit, Michigan

p. 237: Right, lower two images, Courtesy Reilly Architectural, Calverton, New York

pp. 243–247: Courtesy Michael Boucher Landscape Architecture, © MBLA, Freeport, Maine

The publisher gratefully acknowledges permission granted to reproduce the copyrighted materials in this book. Every effort has been made to contact copyright holders and to obtain their permission for the use of copyrighted material. Notification of any additions or corrections that should be incorporated in future reprints or editions of this publication would be greatly appreciated.

BLUE DREAM
AND THE
LEGACY OF
MODERNISM
IN THE
HAMPTONS

Julie at the house

Published by DelMonico Books

Copyright © 2023 DelMonico Books
DelMonico Books
available through ARTBOOK / D.A.P.
75 Broad Street, Suite 630
New York NY 10004
artbook.com
delmonicobooks.com

"Blue Dream and the Legacy of Modernism
in the Hamptons," © Paul Goldberger

Photography portfolio © Iwan Baan

CREATIVE DIRECTOR
Lorraine Wild, Los Angeles
DESIGNERS
Lorraine Wild and Xiaoqing Wang,
Green Dragon Office, Los Angeles
EDITOR
Denise Bratton, Los Angeles
PRODUCTION DIRECTOR
Karen Farquhar, DelMonico Books, New York
COLOR SEPARATIONS
Echelon Color, Santa Monica
RIGHTS AND REPRODUCTIONS
Lilly Leif, Los Angeles

This book is typeset in Dada Grotesk,
designed by deValence, Paris,
published by the Optimo foundry, Geneva

Printed and bound in Italy

Library of Congress Control number
2023933619

ISBN: 978-1-63681-112-3

All rights reserved. No part of this book may be reproduced
or transmitted in any form or by any means, electronic or
mechanical, including photocopying, recording, or any other
information storage and retrieval system, or otherwise
without written permission from the publishers.